CAMBRIDGE LIBRARY COLLECTION

Books of enduring scholarly value

History

The books reissued in this series include accounts of historical events and movements by eye-witnesses and contemporaries, as well as landmark studies that assembled significant source materials or developed new historiographical methods. The series includes work in social, political and military history on a wide range of periods and regions, giving modern scholars ready access to influential publications of the past.

The Opportunity

James Stephen (1758–1832) was a British lawyer and slavery abolitionist. After qualifying for the bar at Lincoln's Inn in 1782 Stephen sailed for St Kitts in 1783. The atrocities committed against slaves which he witnessed in the West Indies converted him to the abolitionist cause, and after his return to England in 1794 he campaigned on behalf of the abolition movement. This volume, first published in 1804, contains Stephen's discussion of Britain's political choices following the successful Haitian Revolution (1791–1804). Before the Revolution, Haiti was one of the wealthiest colonies in the Caribbean, which Britain had attempted unsuccessfully to acquire by force. Stephen explores the complex political situation created by Haiti's declaration of independence, and advocates for Britain to acknowledge Haiti as a sovereign state. Stephen's thorough assessment of Britain's political choices and their potential impact provides valuable insights into contemporary trade and political motivations surrounding Haiti.

Cambridge University Press has long been a pioneer in the reissuing of out-of-print titles from its own backlist, producing digital reprints of books that are still sought after by scholars and students but could not be reprinted economically using traditional technology. The Cambridge Library Collection extends this activity to a wider range of books which are still of importance to researchers and professionals, either for the source material they contain, or as landmarks in the history of their academic discipline.

Drawing from the world-renowned collections in the Cambridge University Library, and guided by the advice of experts in each subject area, Cambridge University Press is using state-of-the-art scanning machines in its own Printing House to capture the content of each book selected for inclusion. The files are processed to give a consistently clear, crisp image, and the books finished to the high quality standard for which the Press is recognised around the world. The latest print-on-demand technology ensures that the books will remain available indefinitely, and that orders for single or multiple copies can quickly be supplied.

The Cambridge Library Collection will bring back to life books of enduring scholarly value (including out-of-copyright works originally issued by other publishers) across a wide range of disciplines in the humanities and social sciences and in science and technology.

The Opportunity

Or Reasons for an Immediate Alliance with St. Domingo

Ｊａｍｅｓ Ｓｔｅｐｈｅｎ

CAMBRIDGE
UNIVERSITY PRESS

CAMBRIDGE UNIVERSITY PRESS

Cambridge, New York, Melbourne, Madrid, Cape Town, Singapore,
São Paolo, Delhi, Dubai, Tokyo, Mexico City

Published in the United States of America by Cambridge University Press, New York

www.cambridge.org
Information on this title: www.cambridge.org/9781108024365

© in this compilation Cambridge University Press 2010

This edition first published 1804
This digitally printed version 2010

ISBN 978-1-108-02436-5 Paperback

OPPORTUNITY,

&c. &c.

THE

OPPORTUNITY;

OR,

REASONS

FOR AN

IMMEDIATE ALLIANCE

WITH

ST. DOMINGO.

———————

BY THE

AUTHOR OF " THE CRISIS OF THE SUGAR COLONIES."

————————————

LONDON:

PRINTED BY C. WHITTINGHAM,
Dean Street, Fetter Lane;

FOR J. HATCHARD, PICCADILLY.

————

1804.

TO THE

RIGHT HON. WILLIAM PITT,

CHANCELLOR OF THE EXCHEQUER, &c. &c.

———————

SIR,

I USE a freedom which may appear a little extraordinary in prefixing your name to a letter originally addressed to Mr. Addington.

To conceal this seeming impropriety, by expunging his name from the following sheets, would not be difficult; for I wrote not to Mr. Addington, but to the Prime Minister of this country : but to make such an alteration in a work already printed, would be to incur two inconveniences —loss of time, which in this case, perhaps, may be important to the public, and loss of money, which you know is rarely unimportant to an author.

This

This work was commenced soon after the evacuation of St. Domingo by the French was first announced in Europe.— The Author, to his surprise, then found reason to suspect, that his Majesty's ministers were irresolute as to the line of policy which it might be expedient to adopt towards the people of that island; and conceiving that by such indecision an opportunity of obtaining much good, and averting great evils, might be irrecoverably lost, he resolved to offer his advice on that interesting subject, both to the Minister and to the Public.

The execution of this purpose, however, was repeatedly interrupted by unavoidable private impediments, and the work has loitered long in the Press, as well as in the closet. One half of the following sheets were printed, and nearly the whole remainder composed, before the late change of administration took place or was expected; and yet it has been impossible to publish them sooner.

Delay, Sir, in these eventful times, is peculiarly inconvenient to statesmen and political writers.

The

The titles and situations of all my principal parties are already become obso-
lete. Mr. Addington is no longer Chancellor of the Exchequer; Buonaparte is
become Emperor of the French; and
Dessalines sole Governor, instead of Tri-
umvir, not of St. Domingo, but Hayti.

But what is more important, the events
which it was my aim to avert are already
beginning to outwing the tardy progress
of my pen and of the press. Dessalines,
if late rumour may be trusted, is not only
acting upon maxims very opposite to those
by which he lately attempted to conciliate
his European neighbours, and perpetrat-
ing crimes which a better policy on our
part might have prevented, but is already
waging that maritime war which was predicted in the following sheets, and de-
nouncing, with a voice far more impres-
sive than mine, the necessity of our restoring peace to the Gulph of Mexico, if we
would avert from it new revolutions. I
must publish without further delay, lest
we should hear next of his having quar-
relled with Jamaica, and conquered Cuba,
or of a reconciliation on the basis of
in-

independency between St. Domingo and France.

Allow me, therefore, Sir, to transfer to you, in its original shape, as an official heir-loom, the advice which was meant for your predecessor.

I have the honour to be,

SIR,

Your most obedient

humble Servant,

THE AUTHOR.

May 31, 1804.

OPPORTUNITY.

SIR,

Near two years ago, I publicly addressed to you some reflections on West Indian affairs, in a pamphlet entitled, The Crisis of the Sugar Colonies.

Had the opinions maintained in that publication been refuted by intermediate events, it would have been unreasonable to expect from you at this period, a favourable or a patient attention; but if, on the contrary, those opinions have been since strikingly verified by experience, I may, without presumption, claim a second audience on the same interesting subject.

Nor will it weaken this pretension, if you should be able to recollect, that the author's views were thought on their first promulgation, to be singular, and his practical conclusions rash: for the tes-

B   timony

timony of experience in their favour is not the less decisive; and when political suggestions are demonstrated to have been just, their singularity and apparent boldness become arguments of their necessity and importance.

Unless vanity deceive me, that publication, however diffidently received by yourself or your colleagues, was not wholly fruitless of some important public effects.

Though personally a stranger to you, I know that you honoured the work with a perusal; and would hope that it contributed in some degree to fix you in a line of conduct in what relates to St. Domingo, from which you have had much excitement to swerve, but of which the wisdom as well as the rectitude, is now universally acknowledged.

If so, my claim to your patient attention rests upon a still stronger title than that which has been already advanced.

To my former advice, much popular prepossession certainly stood opposed; and as I have now to offer further counsel, suggested by the same views, to which, perhaps, in some points, the current of public opinion may still be adverse, a brief retrospect of some of the leading opinions maintained in "The Crisis," and of the experimental confirmation which they have received, may be no improper or unnecessary prelude.

After

After offering many reasons for believing that
the ostensible purpose held out by the French
government was not its real object in the great
expedition then proceeding againt St. Domingo,
but that the restitution of private slavery was the
Consul's true purpose, I endeavoured in that pamphlet to point out the peculiar obstacles, both physical and moral, by which the accomplishment of
that purpose would be opposed *

In delineating these, it was found necessary to
adduce facts relative to colonial slavery, of which
the true nature was generally misconceived in
Europe †; and here, to some minds celebrated
for political knowledge in general, as well as to
many ordinary readers, the author's premises, as
he has reason to believe, appeared not less ques-
tionable than his conclusions : yet, reasoning
from these premises, he inferred with much confidence the high probability of events which
have since actually occurred in St. Domingo,
extraordinary and wonderful though those events
have appeared to the European public ‡. The
harsh and unparalleled nature of West India
bondage in general, and those distinguishing
features of that state which were delineated in
the Crisis, were the very corner stones, and

* Crisis, Letter 2d.
† Ib. p. 7 to 15.
‡ Ib. p. 56 to 76.

foundation

foundation walls, upon the solidity of which the whole structure of the argument depended.

From the terrible peculiarities of that state, and from these alone, it was inferred, that the negroes of St. Domingo would never submit to it again*; for it was admitted, that to any yoke known elsewhere by the name of slavery, the gigantic power, the relentless vengeance, the craft, and violence of the French government, might probably be able to enforce submission. Political, and even personal freedom had been completely overthrown in many parts of Europe; and there was nothing in the air of the Antilles to make the spirit of liberty there more vigorous, or less tameable by the terror of the sword; but it was predicted that negro freedom would be found invincible in St. Domingo, because the horrors of the state opposed to it were experimentally known to its defenders: and because they were of that intolerable kind which the author endeavoured to describe†. He foresaw the true though strange issue of the unequal contest between the colossal republic of France, and the negroes of a West India island, only because he clearly understood the nature of the practical question in dispute.

The great local and personal advantages,

* Crisis, p. 55-6.
† Ib. p. 46 to 56, 75-6, &c

which

which favoured the cause of freedom in that climate, were not overlooked or concealed—on the
contrary, they were fully explained and relied
upon * as necessary means ; but the vital and in-
domitable principle, which could alone give life
and efficacy to those means of resistance, was an
aversion to the former yoke not to be overcome ;
an antipathy more powerful, than all the terrors
that despotism could oppose to it, more stimu-
lating than any passion or appetite that could
plead for submission, and more obstinate than the
love of life itself.

Upon these premises and these calculations, it
was foretold early in March, 1802, that the issue
of the French expedition would be such as, to the
astonishment of Europe, it has ultimately proved—
disappointment to the views of the consul, and a
triumph to his sable opponents.

In the progress and incidents, as well as the
final event of that extraordinary contest, the
" Crisis of the Sugar Colonies" has proved for the
most part a history by anticipation of the war
of St. Domingo.

That the arms of France would probably have
a short-lived apparent success was foreseen † ; nor

* Crisis, p. 58 to 69.
† Ib. p. 44-5.

were

were the artifices and frauds, which concurred with force in the attainment of that ephemeral triumph, unexpected *; but it was also foreseen that the discovery of the true object of the war would produce a new and decisive resistance †.

The facility, so clearly manifested, of obtaining a loyal submission to the republic without the restitution of the former slavery ‡; the speedy resort to a compromise on that basis, such as was actually, though perfidiously, made by Leclerc, after force had been tried in vain § ; the division of the negro chiefs and troops, by a crafty concealment of the design against freedom in the outset, and the consequent defection of many of them from Toussaint ‖ ; their faithful adherence, nevertheless, to the cause of general freedom, when the mask was dropped by the invaders ¶ ; these, and other leading incidents of the contest, were all foretold in the Crisis, with more or less confidence and clearness, in proportion as they were more or less necessary results of the general premises from which they were all inferred.

To point out at large the agreement of these

* Crisis, p. 45.
† Ib. p. 45-6.
‡ Ib. p. 45.
§ Ib. p. 85.
‖ Ib. p. 45.
¶ Ib. p. 45-6. 56-7, 8.

conjectural

conjectural conclusions with subsequent events, would be to exceed those limits, which regard to your time, Sir, and my own, must prescribe to this address. The task will be more easy when a tolerably fair and intelligent account of the late war in St. Domingo shall meet the public eye; but in spite of the unprecedented falshood of the consular press, no Englishman is so ill informed of the events of that horrible war, as not to perceive, should he now turn over the pages of the Crisis, that the opinions there disclosed have been fully verified, and the author's expectations very strikingly confirmed.

To the purpose for which this brief review is offered, the confirmation of the premises of fact contained in that pamphlet, some events unforeseen by the author, are no less important than those which his conjectures embraced.

That a compromise would be the result of the obstinate resistance which the French generals would encounter, and of their despair of final success, he foresaw to be probable *; but that perfidy so unexampled in the history of this bad world, as was practised by the French commanders, would be employed to frustrate the compact, was as much beyond his foresight as that of the illustrious victim of the crime, the generous and immortal Toussaint. Ignorant of the yet

* Crisis, p. 85.

unfathomed

unfathomed depth of French depravity, and supposing that the consul had more political wisdom than he has lately exhibited, the author did not foresee the probability of a measure, at once the basest and the weakest that ever dishonoured a nation. The second jeopardy, therefore, to the cause of African freedom, which resulted from this perfidy, put the strength of the defensive principle and means, upon which the author relied, to a proof unexpectedly severe : yet such were the truth and the force of those premises upon which his reasoning was built, so invincible were the feelings which withstood the restitution of slavery, and such the natural means of resistance, that the betrayed and disheartened colonists, though perfidiously deprived of their leaders, of their military champions, and of their arms, again made head against the armies of the republic, and again triumphed over their powerful and ferocious oppressors.

The desperate perseverance with which the war was afterwards prosecuted by the consul, the terrible means which he employed, and the remorseless devotion of the monsters Leclerc and Rochambeau, and their troops, to their master's horrible behests, were also far beyond the author's calculations ; but the principles upon which he relied have passed unhurt through all these extreme ordeals, and their justice has by every trial been more clearly established.

The

The last and strongest confirmation has been given by the consul himself. He, who acted upon notions diametrically opposite to the opinions maintained in the Crisis, and who expected so little difficulty in the execution of his projects, that he sent not only his brother, and brother-in-law, but his sister, with her infant child, to grace and enjoy his expected easy triumph over African freedom, saw at length his error so clearly, that in despair of re-establishing slavery, he resolved on extermination; and instead of still aiming to reclaim a flourishing colony, fought, massacred, and murdered for a desert.

Without detaining you longer with a review, to the seeming egotism of which I could be reconciled only by its undeniable public importance, I demand in general new credence to the facts, and some increased regard to the conclusions contained in my former address; to some of which I shall have occasion to revert in the course of the ensuing discussions. In particular, I hope that one great truth, which was matter of argumentative induction in the Crisis, the invincibility of freedom in St. Domingo, may now be fairly assumed, as a proved and incontestible truth.

The new and interesting question which I propose now to discuss, is " *what line of conduct a* " *British minister ought, at the present juncture,* " *to adopt towards the people of St. Domingo ?*"

C   Upon

Upon this important question, but one practical notion, and that of a very indefinite kind, seems as yet to have entered into the conception of the public. That every degree of amity towards this new society, consistent with a due regard to our own colonial interests, ought to be observed, seems to be a unanimous sentiment. It seems also to be in general thought, that some commercial intercourse ought to be formed with them, so as to secure to ourselves whatever trade their industry may immediately furnish. But these opinions, as far as they have met the public eye, are qualified by so many cautious and ambiguous terms, that their authors may be affirmed to have yet formed no decisive practical judgment.

For my part, having a distinct and firm opinion on this interesting subject, an opinion, which, however erroneous it may be, is simple, practical, and, in my own poor judgment, highly important to my country, I feel myself bound to declare it ; and shall do so without management or reserve.

YOU OUGHT, SIR, I CONCEIVE TO ACKNOWLEDGE WITHOUT DELAY, THE LIBERTY OF THE NEGROES OF ST. DOMINGO ; AND TO ENTER INTO FŒDERAL ENGAGEMENTS WITH THEM AS A SOVEREIGN AND INDEPENDENT PEOPLE; AND YOU OUGHT FURTHER, NOT ONLY TO GRANT, BUT, IF NECESSARY, TO VOLUNTEER, A GUARANTEE OF THEIR INDEPENDENCY AGAINST THE REPUBLIC OF FRANCE.

Should this proposition startle at first by its apparent

parent boldness, it is no more than I expect. So let me again hint, did the opinion maintained in the Crisis, that the colossal Republic of France, the terror of continental Europe, could not with all its force, crush this same petty community of negroes. So it might be added, did at its first promulgation, almost every opinion or measure of national policy, which in this age of wonders has ultimately proved to have been wise. These are times in which hesitating choice and tardy decision will generally be found at a fault, and in which a British statesman should remember Cato's maxim, that

"———— Fear admitted into public councils
" Betrays like treason."————

But should you favour me with a patient attention, you will perhaps find that the course here proposed, though a decided, is not a rash one : that the measures I recommend are bold in appearance only, not in reality; and, that they are in truth essential to any plan of colonial policy, from which future security can be expected or hoped.

Let not my advice be prejudged at the outset by that dislike of innovation in the abstract, which the experience of the age has inspired. A new order of things has arisen in the West Indies, to which former precedents are quite inapplicable. The British statesman has there no beaten path to pursue; he has a new country before him, and

a new

a new road to explore. An unprecedented re-volution has rent asunder the basis of our old Colonial policy, and further perseverance in it, out of mere respect to its antiquity, would savour more of pedantry than prudence : its former wisdom, had it indeed been wise, would perhaps be the clearest evidence of its future folly.

It was, I grant, a fundamental maxim of all the powers of Europe who possessed colonies in the Antilles, that the supremacy of the European race, and the depression of the African, must be at all times, and at the expence of every other public principle, maintained. It was a rule paramount in importance to all national rivalships, and to all national quarrels. There was an intercommunity of feelings and privileges among the white skinned colonists, which, when the subordination of negroes was in question, made English and French, Dutch and Spanish, European friend and European enemy, very unimportant distinctions.

But this strong chain of sympathy, forged by mutuality of despotic abuse, and rivetted by a sense of common danger, has been broken by the same shock that overthrew the social edifices of Europe; and effects have followed, of which the stability can now no more be doubted, than the novelty or the importance.

An African people, insubordinated to any
European

European inhabitants of the same territory, and independent of all exterior government, is planted in the centre of the Antilles; and possesses an entire island, the most important of the group* : An island of far greater extent than any other (Cuba alone excepted) in the whole Western Archipelago, and which, in population and produce, was lately equal to all the rest united.

This new society has already proved itself, in its very infancy, unconquerable by the greatest powers in the civilized world, having successively defended its freedom and its territory against the long continued hostility of Great Britain at one period; and against the vast, impetuous, persevering, and merciless, efforts of France at another. By power and victory, therefore, as well as by freedom and independency, is the African race raised from its late prostrate and despised state in this very considerable part of the West Indies. Instead of that abject and brutal condition which was before their universal lot, the black islanders may now reasonably elevate their heads above their palefaced neighbours; for whether their country shall remain permanently severed from

* The language of an old historian of this island is remarkable: " *La situation de cette isle par rapport aux autres* " *Antilles, ne pouvoit etre plus avantageuse.   Elle en est presque* " *environée, & l'on diroit qu' élle à été placée au centre de ce* " *grand Archipel pour lui donner la loi.*"   Hist. de L'isle Espagnole par Charlevoix, Tom. I. Liv. i.

France

the dominion of France or not ; it possesses a potential independency, of which none of its neighbours can boast : while they continue to lean for support and protection upon distant states, St. Domingo is found to be able not only to sustain itself without the aid of those states, but to set the greatest of them at defiance.

To persist after so extreme a revolution, in our anterior policy, would be more irrational, than even to retain the prejudices by which that policy was introduced and upheld. If we can be so far the dupes of prepossession as still to hold these sable heroes and patriots personally cheap, let us at least respect their power ; and advert to the danger of still acting towards them upon principles of Creolian antipathy and contempt.

National prejudice may indeed, in this case, as in others, survive the causes from which it was derived ; but a wise statesman will, in such cases, rather veer round with the refluent tide of events, than vainly attempt to stem it, by still courting the lingering breeze of opinion. Rome had not ceased, perhaps, in the days of Honorius to despise the northern barbarians ; but Stilicho was not absurd enough to disdain to treat with those hardy warriors, upon Roman ground; or to apply to them in other respects the old imperial maxims. At this day we regard, with just derision, the arrogant and contemptuous style of the impotent

successors

successors of Othman; but though they call us,
" Christian dogs," they are too prudent to adhere in their public councils, to a correspondent
practice. They thankfully accept us as allies, and
are happy to secure the patrimony of the pro-
phet by our unhallowed aid.

Though revolution in this case touches only
the skirts of the empire, the principle of policy
is the same; and let not the British cabinet display more bigotry, and less wisdom, in the western
Archipelago, than the Turkish Divan, or Grand
Vizier, in the eastern.

An entire and absolute adherence to our ancient
policy in the Antilles, will scarcely however now
be thought advisable, even by the most prejudiced
mind. The necessity of a material departure from
it has indeed, been practically admitted, in many
measures of the last and present war; especially
in our convention with Toussaint, and in the
assistance lately given to his successors against
their European enemies : for such measures, wise
and necessary though they must be allowed to
have been, were directly at variance with the
policy adhered to at all former periods.

But prejudice, though obliged to abandon its
former lines, may be disposed in this case to make
only a partial and lingering retreat. Though it
is demonstrably unwise still to treat the new people as natural inferiors and enemies, it may to
many,

many, seem a boldness of innovation to treat them
as independent equals and friends. Of this hesitating sentiment, I am sorry to perceive strong
symptoms in our late conduct on the coast of St.
Domingo. My advice, therefore, may possibly still
be opposed by some adverse prepossession on the
score of novelty. If obliged to innovate, let us, it
may be said, be slow and cautious in the process.

But let it well be considered, that the circumstances out of which our colonial policy arose, are
not merely altered; they are completely reversed.
From universal bondage in the Antilles, the
African race, I repeat, has started into liberty,
sovereignty, and power. Instead of subjection to
the lowest of foreign states, they have triumphed
over the most powerful. A correspondent reverse has also, in a more important point, been
adopted in the conduct of this and other nations.
To that close confederacy of the European race in
the Antilles, by which the chains of the negroes
seemed to be for ever rivetted, have succeeded
wars between European powers, in which these
once despised objects of the common hostility
and oppression have been received as auxiliaries
and co-belligerents at least, if not also as allies.
The change, so far as regards the queen of the
West Indian islands, the sole subject of these re-
marks, is, in all points, perfect and extreme.
Now if different situations, require different measures,

sures; opposite situations, seem to demand opposite measures. But at least, it can furnish no
sound presumption against the wisdom of a new
system of conduct, that it is diametrically opposite
to former principles, when the case itself has been
totally reversed; and this is all for which I wish
at present to contend.

Let us proceed then to consider, without any
prepossession or bias, the arguments by which
the advice I have offered may be fairly recommended or opposed.

The first step towards a right choice, is to sur-
vey attentively the different objects among which
we have to chuse: and as it seems to me, that
in this case there are, in a general view, but four
different paths of conduct, in one of which you
must of necessity tread, it may be proper to say
something of each. They are,

1st. To interdict all commercial intercourse
whatever, between his Majesty's subjects and the
people of St. Domingo.

2d. To permit such intercourse, but without
any conventional basis.

3d. To enter into some commercial treaty or
convention with the negro chiefs, not involving
any relations closer than those of general amity
and trade.

4th. To adopt the decisive measures which I
have ventured to recommend.

Of

Of the first of these plans little perhaps need be said, for it will probably find few, if any, supporters.

Such a measure would in the first place be-found to be attended with great practical difficulties. The advantages of the prohibited trade, and the facility of a clandestine intercourse between St. Domingo and Jamaica, would probably give rise to an extensive contraband commerce. Every view of political caution upon which the prohibition could be founded, would in that case be defeated ; for if a trade with this new people, though lawfully and openly conducted, would be dangerous to our colonies, a secret, illicit, and consequently unregulated intercourse, could not be less so.

But the prohibition, whether abortive or effectual, would be very likely to produce a consequence which every reflecting mind must strongly deprecate. A total interdiction of trade between British subjects and the inhabitants of St. Domingo, could not well consist, in the notions of the latter, with the belief of a pacific disposition on our part, and would naturally incline them to regard us as secret foes to their freedom as well as their independence.

Besides, the strong means by which alone such a prohibition could be enforced, would look too much like war, not to be easily mistaken for it, by a people inexpert in political distinctions, and
justly

justly jealous of the disposition of all their more civilized neighbours.

But supposing this line of policy to be open to no such practical objections, it involves a sacrifice of advantages, which this commercial and maritime country ought not, without very important reasons, to make.

The ports of St. Domingo, notwithstanding all the desolations of the late dreadful war, and the wasteful effects of foreign and intestine calamities during nine or ten preceding years, will still have some valuable exports to furnish. The captures made of cargoes shipped from that island since the commencement of the present hostilities, sufficiently prove that agriculture, however diminished, had not been wholly abandoned ; much less will the hoe be idle when the musket may be safely laid aside ; for that freedom and a negro government are not incompatible with a large and increasing growth of exportable produce, was, under the beneficent administration of Toussaint*, very clearly proved.

The

* The exports from St. Domingo, throughout the last war, however small when compared to their former amount, were by no means contemptible. But under the government of Toussaint, especially after his treaty with General Maitland had relieved him from the severe pressure of a maritime war, the tillage of the island was rapidly improving. The French commanders on the arrival of their ill fated expedition,

The barbarous and impolitic measures of the consul, have unquestionably occasioned a vast deterioration in the state of the colony since that fortunate period, in respect not only of immediate produce, but of the works and buildings necessary in the manufacturing of sugar; but of so great and fertile a field even the gleanings must be important; and there is no good reason for doubting that its prosperity will speedily revive.

tion, were surprised to find agriculture in so high a degree restored. " The cultivation of the colony," said Leclerc, in his first official dispatches, " *is in a much higher state of pros-* " *perity than could have been imagined.*" Official dispatches of February 9th, 1802, in London newspapers of March 26th.

Upon this head, the word of the French government or its commanders may safely be taken; because the exaggeration of existing prosperity, would have magnified the merit of the man, whom they had recently proscribed as a traitor; and tended strongly to recommend an order of things, which they were labouring by the most dreadful means to abolish.

An equally unexceptionable testimony of the same tendency, lately met the author's eye, in a letter found on board *Le Bon Accord, Pierre Patissier, master,* a prize taken at the commencement of the present war. The writer, who appears to be a very intelligent Frenchman, and to have been commanding engineer at Port au Prince, and who addresses himself confidentially to a superior officer of his own corps in France, in speaking of the recent battles and conflagrations in the south of the island, says: " *La partie du sud, qui* IL Y A " DEUX MOIS ET DEMI *etoit encore intacte* ET VALAIT MIEUX, QUE " LA MARTINIQUE, TANT PAR SON ETENDUE, QUE PAR SES RAPPORTS, " *est maintenant le theatre de la guerre la plus horrible,* &c."

The original letter is in the Registry of the High Court of Admiralty: it is dated at the Cape, 18 Floreal, An. 11. (May 7, 1803.)

That

That the produce of the island will soon be as great as it was before the revolution, is, I admit, more than can be reasonably expected. The number of adults fit for labour is unquestionably reduced in a very great proportion ; nor will free men and women ever be brought to work so intensely as slaves are compelled to do by the coercion of the whip. They will not labour more severely than consists with the preservation of health, with the ordinary duration of life, and the maintenance and increase of native population ; which is only saying in other words what is expressed in the preceding sentence.

But unless new demons should arise to re-act the madness of Buonaparte, the effects of the new system will, in a few years, amply make up for this double drawback on the immediate efforts of the planter. The superfecundity of unoppressed human nature, will not only give back what the sword and the drownings have destroyed, but will produce rapidly an overflowing population ; and husbandry will regain in the number of labourers, what it loses by mitigation of toil *.

Whatever

* M. Malouet's information on these subjects must have been more copious and authoritative than that of almost any other man in Europe; for in addition to his long experience in colonial affairs, and extensive private acquaintance in the West Indian circles, he, as the public apologist of the Consul, had access, no doubt, to the official correspondence and other papers in the bureaus

Whatever the amount of the exportable produce of this great island may be, its import of foreign commodities will be as great at least as the barter of that produce may suffice to purchase; and its export, as well as import trade, will long be entirely carried on in foreign shipping, and on account of foreign merchants: for it would be extravagant to suppose, that this new community of husbandmen and soldiers, will soon acquire a trading capital of its own, or a commercial marine.

No branch of commerce which we possess, can in its kind be more desirable than this to a manufacturing and maritime country. Its value in a national view will, in proportion to its actual extent, very far exceed that of our present West Indian trade: for the ships which bring over the produce of our islands, do not, upon an average, obtain one-third of an entire freight on their outward voyages; and for this obvious reason, that a small proportion only of the proceeds of the imported colonial

reaus of the colonial department. The following testimony of M. Malouet is therefore of great importance. " *Tous les rapports annoncent un beaucoup plus grand nombre d'enfans, et moins de mortalité parmis les negrillons, qu'il n'y en avoit avant la revolution: ce qui est imputé au repos absolu dont jouissent les femmes grosses, et a un moi ndre travail de la part des négres.*" (Collection de Memoirs sur les Colonies, &c. par V. P. Malouet, ancien Administrateur des Colonies et de la Marine, Tome IV. Introduction, p. 52.) M. Malouet, let it be observed, is no *ami des noirs*, but a West Indian, and a defender of the Slave Trade.

produce

produce is sent back in European goods, perhaps not a twentieth part *; whereas these new customers would lay out in our manufactures nearly the whole net value of their sugar and coffee, or rather would barter those tropical products in their own ports, for the goods of Birmingham and Manchester, giving us the carriage of both.

This important consideration cannot be fully discussed without exceeding the limits which must be prescribed to the present publication; but to the reflections of any well informed and dispassionate mind, it will be obvious that such views are by no means chimerical; and that a thousand hogsheads of sugar brought from the ports of St. Domingo, would perhaps be the medium of more substantial benefit to the manufacturers, merchants, and ship owners of Great Britain, collectively considered, than five thousand from St. Kitt's or Jamaica; with this most important difference, that the former branch of trade would

---

* The rum made on a sugar plantation, of which but a small part is brought to Europe, sometimes defrays all the ordinary expences of the estate. Generally speaking, however, one-tenth part of the proceeds of the sugar is computed to be a necessary auxiliary fund, to supply deficiencies, and provide for contingencies ; but this, for the most part, is applied by the consignees in paying bills drawn by the planter for the purchase of American goods and other colonial expences, and therefore forms no part of the returns in European investment and freight.

not

not involve as a drawback upon its advantages, any part of that enormous expence of life and treasure by which our West Indian colonies are protected.

It is needless to dwell on the importance ot inducements, like these; for they are in their nature, considerations to which the people of this country are more than sufficiently awake, and to which from a British Minister, I should rather in general fear too eager and exclusive an attention, than any improper indifference.

An inevitable consequence, on the other hand, of our abstaining from this commerce, would be its falling into the hands of other powers, who would have no motive for a similar sacrifice; and here the commercial jealousy of the nation will be also sufficiently quicksighted and apprehensive, without any argumentative excitement. But the importance of this consideration is still greater in a political, than in a commercial view, as I shall soon have occasion to shew. At present, I will not enlarge upon this topic, as its discussion more properly belongs to a subsequent branch of my subject.

The arguments which may be opposed to the permission of commerce with this new people, can only, I conceive, be drawn from the dangers to which our own islands may be exposed by it.

That the new state of St. Domingo will be perilous to our sugar colonies, unless great and

speedy

speedy reformation shall meliorate their own interior system, it is far from my intention to deny. The danger is real and great, and, as I have elsewhere endeavoured to demonstrate*, calls loudly for preventative measures from the government and parliament of Great Britain. Unhappily no such measures have hitherto been adopted; and therefore though the folly and wickedness of Buonaparte have, fortunately for this country, suspended the progress of the danger, and diminished its immediate magnitude, our colonies, Jamaica especially, are unquestionably still in very serious jeopardy. But that the cause of alarm would be lessened by our avoiding all amicable relations with the negro chiefs, and holding towards them a face of jealous dislike, is a proposition which it would be difficult to maintain.

Among the many advantages which the apologists of the slave trade have taken of the misconceptions naturally prevalent in Europe, respecting the true nature and effects of West Indian bondage, an outcry was raised by them on the score of alleged dangers from the speeches and writings of abolitionists; which, they pretended, would reach the ears of the enslaved negroes, and inspire them with revolutionary notions. With equal gravity, " *the vir-*" *tuous Le Clerc,*" declaimed, amidst the details of his destructive campaign, against the "mis-

* Crisis, p. 79, 80-124, &c.

E   " chiefs

" chiefs of *abstract principles* *." Were such
ideas sincere and well founded, or were not these
poor degraded beings placed by their incessant
labour, by the domestic police of the plantations,
and still more by that dulness and stupidity to
which a brutalizing oppression has reduced them,
below the reach of the revolutionary means
used by the Jacobins of Europe, I admit that
a commercial intercourse with St. Domingo might
be no less dangerous to Jamaica, than a hostile disposition in these new and formidable neighbours.
Their acquaintance might, even in that case, be
more perilous than their hatred. But to those who
know the true state and character of those op-
pressed fellow beings, such grounds of apprehension are not very alarming; and as to the dread
of democratical or revolutionary theories being employed to excite disaffection in a gang of field
negroes, a West Indian could not hear of such a
notion without laughing; unless indeed it were
in England, where policy might induce him in
such a case to do violence to his risible muscles. To
him, such fears must appear scarcely less ridiculous,
than those of a waggoner, who having read the
voyage to the Hhuynhymms, should dread the
effects upon the temper of his team, of a democratical song from the ostler.

* See his dispatches of February 9th, 1802. London Papers
of March 24.

It

It is in truth, through the new means of physical force, not those of political suggestion or intrigue, that the propagation of freedom from the neighbouring coast of St. Domingo, is really to be apprehended at Jamaica. Hostility, therefore, in the breasts of the new people, and not an amicable connection with them, should be the subject of anxious prevention.

For the justice of these views, more fully explained in my former pamphlet, I might appeal to our experience during the whole of the last war; for if precept or example could have excited insurrection among our slaves, those means were never wanting to the enemy; and revolutionary freedom was exhibited for many years in a living model of grand dimensions under the very windows of some of our colonies, especially at Montserrat and Jamaica; yet no insurrection took place among the slaves of those islands; nor was the contagion felt for a moment any where, except where it was carried by hostile force.

But more satisfactory proof how innoxious the new system is in the way of pacific intercourse, may be found in the conduct of those who are most interested in, as well as best acquainted with the subject. The planters of Jamaica are a body not inattentive to their own peculiar interests in public measures, nor badly represented in this country. Have you then, Sir, had any
                                        application

application from them to prohibit a trade with St. Domingo? If so, they have strangely altered their views since the last war; for such an intercourse was openly carried on between the two islands to a great extent, after the convention with Toussaint; and not a murmur against it was heard, either from the assembly of Jamaica, or from the very active West Indian committee. It was, on the contrary, so favourite a branch of commerce in that island, that the restrictions which the royal prudence had imposed upon it, for the sake apparently of diminishing the dangers in question *, were there thought to shackle too strictly the profitable intercourse with St. Domingo ; and were so broadly violated in the face of day, that English ships, belonging to the ports of Jamaica, were seized by his Majesty's squadron, and confiscated for that cause †. When we next hear of danger to the peace of our islands, from the speeches of abolitionists, I hope these facts will be remembered.

Were the intercourse in question really dangerous to our sugar colonies, there would be no necessity either to expose them to any such peril, or to forego, for their sakes, the national advantages

* Order in Council of 9th January, 1799.

† Case of the Achilles, —— Sutherland, master, heard before the Lords Commissioners of Appeals in Prize Causes, March 3d, 1804.

of

of the trade; for we have ports, even in the West
Indies, from which the commerce might be carried
on, without producing any such political inconvenience. On this hint I propose to enlarge
hereafter. Meantime, supposing enough to have
been already said to prove that the commerce
which courts our acceptance ought not to be
wholly declined, and believing that thus far my
opinion is that of the public at large, I will proceed
to consider the second of the four projects proposed for discussion: " That of allowing trade to
" be carried on with the negroes of St. Domingo
" without any conventional basis."

This scheme has certainly more practical facility
than the former: but if it be admitted that a commercial intercourse of any kind ought to be allowed,
it will, I conceive, be difficult to deny, that it ought
to be sanctioned and regulated by some express
compact.

If in the mercantile intercourse of civilized
and polished nations, positive conventions are
found useful or necessary, in order to prevent disputes, to obviate inconveniencies, and to improve
the mutual advantage, surely they cannot be less
so in this case, in which, supposing disputes to arise,
there are with one of the parties no precedents or
known principles, by which they could be decided.

By a treaty with the negro chiefs, better assur-
ance

ance might be obtained, for the observance of mercantile faith, and for the security of British subjects in their property and their persons, while trading in the ports of a country, still perhaps likely to be the seat of much interior disorder. By a treaty also, regulations might be framed whereby such political inconveniencies and hazards as must be in some degree incident to this new branch of commerce, might be materially lessened. Particular ports for instance might be limited, as in his Majesty's order of council for licensing the trade with Toussaint's government, or in the West Indian free port acts, which in like manner innovated upon the general restrictions of our maritime code, and in which it was therefore found necessary to provide many precautions against the probable ill effects of innovation.

Fiscal, as well as political, regulations, would obviously, on our side, be necessary ; but without a treaty the most salutary and necessary sanctions in laws of that kind, might in their execution, give umbrage to these unenlightened neighbours. It may be added, that by mutual agreement only could adequate security be obtained against some dangerous abuses, and sources of future contention, such as the carrying off negroes, to which there would be strong temptations on both sides,

But a still more powerful argument for a commercial

mercial treaty is, that without a compact, we can have no permanent privilege or favour in the ports of that island.

We are now in a situation to become not only the most favoured nation at St. Domingo, but even perhaps to obtain from this new people a monopoly of their trade ; for we who alone can defy the resentment of France, can alone venture to contract with them at this critical period any fœderal relations. Herein consists one material advantage of that opportunity, to which I invite your attention.

The considerations which we must probably give for such exclusive privileges, will be pointed out under the next head of discussion. At present, I would only remark that a treaty of some kind, is the necessary medium of such an important acquisition ; and that if we are content with a mere tacit allowance of general trade, we shall be rivalled by other powers ; and soon, in consequence of the advantages of neutral navigation now possessed by them, shall be undersold and virtually excluded from this valuable branch of commerce. We shall gratuitously relinquish in favour of America, Denmark, and Sweden a great, and perhaps hereafter an inestimable boon, which the circumstances of the present war, as some compensation for its evils, happily throw within our reach.

North America bids fairest to be our great rival

val in the future trade of St. Domingo; but as
the injured islanders have seen the American flag
bringing supplies to their oppressors, during the
deepest horrors of the late dreadful contest, they
can at this moment have no predilection for the
people of that country; while our present hostility to the Republic, and the assistance we have
given in blockading the French armies in their
ports, must dispose them very favourably towards
ourselves *. Supposing we should acquiesce, as it
might be necessary to do, in their importing from
North America some articles of provisions and
lumber, they would, I doubt not, readily give
to our merchants exclusively, the benefit of sup-
plying them with all other commodities.

Extend your view, Sir, to that future complete
restitution of the agriculture of this vast island,
which is at least a possible, and in my poor judgment, no improbable, or distant event. Reflect,
that upon such a restitution, we might import
from St. Domingo alone, far more in bulk and
value of the rich tropical productions than all the
other islands in the West Indies now collectively

* If there should be some abatement of this disposition at
present, from our conduct, in destroying or carrying away
their means of defence at Fort Dauphin, the policy of
which I am by no means able to comprehend, the favourable
sentiment might, by means hereafter to be noticed, be easily
and fully restored.

afford,

afford, and have a million or more of new trans-
atlantic customers to lay out in our manufactures
nearly the whole value of their produce ; and then
ask yourself whether such prospects as these, with
such present benefits in advance, ought to be
wantonly or for slight reasons renounced ? Reject
them at this moment, and they will certainly be
lost for ever.

But it may be asked, what effectual security
would be derived from a treaty for the preservation
of any privileges which it might concede? I answer,
in the first place, that of a faith which there is
no good reason to distrust, for it has hitherto been
unviolated, though strongly tried during the last
war, the faith of this new community. Rude nations, perhaps, are not the least observant of such
engagements. You would, however, have the additional and ever growing security of established
custom ; for they would soon become habitually
partial to our manufactures, and our modes of
commerce: but what is a much stronger ground
of reliance, their self-interest, their love of freedom,
and their abhorrence of a dreadful slavery, would
bind them to your side ; for a guarantee of their
liberty must, as I shall presently show, be the price
of the supposed concessions.

To all these probable advantages of a commercial treaty, there does not seem to stand opposed

F   any

any sound objection which would not at least equally apply to the project now under review.

The countenance and support given to the new order of things would be substantially the same, and the actual intercourse with the people strictly so, whether our trade to their ports were carried on with, or without, any conventional basis.

I will here dismiss the consideration of the second plan, and pass to the third.

3d. " To enter into some treaty or convention " with the negro chiefs, not involving any rela- " tions closer than those of general amity and " commerce."

This is probably the scheme of policy which will at first view appear the most plausible.

" We ought not, it may be conceded, to ab- " stain from the advantages which a trade to " St. Domingo may afford, or contract the suspi- " cion and odium of its new masters, by pro- " hibiting an amicable intercourse between their " territories and our own; we may even pru- " dently and advantageously form with them a " commercial treaty ; but care should be taken " not expressly to recognise their independency, " nor to enter into any stipulations which may be " found inconvenient in a future pacification with " France."

As these views may be thought to derive some

recommendation

recommendation from their seeming conformity
to the policy adopted during the last war in our
convention with Toussaint, I would in the first
place remark, that the precedent is quite inapplicable; for between the leading circumstances of that
case, and of the present, there is not only great
diversity, but a direct and manifest opposition.

At no time prior to the peace of 1801, was there
an opportunity of separating the cause of negro
liberty from that of French ambition, had we been
disposed to adopt that policy. When, by evacuat-
ing St. Domingo, we ceased to make war against
the sable defenders of that island, a great majority
of them were indeed disposed to become our
friends and our commercial customers, but no party
among them evinced any disposition to become
our general allies, or our confederates against the
republic. In a considerable part of the island, where
General Rigaud commanded, hostility to this country continued to prevail almost to the end of the
war; and Toussaint himself, was so far from choos-
ing to engage with us as a confederate, that he
maintained strictly the duties of neutrality. Though
imperious necessity justified in his eyes, and even
in the opinion of the French government, the pacific convention which he made with an enemy of
the mother country, he never ceased to acknowledge her sovereignty, and governed the colony in
right

[36]

right of successive commissions from the immediate rulers of France.

Had we at that period offered a guarantee of liberty and independency, it would in all probability have been rejected ; for the republic, let it be remembered, had not then violated the law by which she had recognised the freedom of her colonial negroes, nor shewn any disposition to restore the ancient system.

But such measures as I now recommend, would, during the last war, have been, on other accounts also, clearly unwise. That France, when released from the restraints imposed upon her by a continental and maritime war, would attempt a counter-revolution in that great colony, was at least probable ; and that the remains of half a million of uncivilized people, after ten years of revolution and war, would be able to effect in the new world what confederated nations had vainly attempted in the old, by repelling the undivided efforts of that gigantic republic, was an opinion, upon the justice of which a statesman could not safely rely. If it appeared a speculation too bold even in the page of a political pamphlet, to build upon it in the practical deliberations of a cabinet would have been highly imprudent.

A chance, therefore, seemed to remain of the restitution in St. Domingo of the system to which

we

we were determined to adhere in our own colonies; and wilfully to exclude it, would, on our existing maxims of policy, have been inconsistent and absurd. But could even the event of the contest have been with certainty foreseen, it would have been thought bad policy to prevent an attempt by which the armies and the resources of France were to be wasted, and the immediate population of St. Domingo at the same time materially reduced ; and, what is of far greater importance, by which the attachment of the black colonists to the republic, might be converted into enmity and detestation.

The invincible stability of the new order of things in St. Domingo, and the opportunity of effectually separating that important island from the dominion of France, are essential foundations of my present advice ; but of these the former was unknown during the last war, and the latter did not exist.

ı. Since then the project now under discussion can claim no sound recommendation from precedent, let us proceed to examine its intrinsic pretensions to your choice.

If I have thus far reasoned justly, we are already arrived at the conclusion, that a trade with St. Domingo ought not to be wholly declined, and that it should be placed on the basis of some commercial treaty to be made with the negro chiefs. It remains, therefore, next to consider whether

commercial

commercial arrangements should be the only objects embraced by such a treaty, or whether it
ought to extend to relations of a closer and more
comprehensive nature.

There is obviously no middle point between a
commercial treaty, which necessarily implies perfect
amity between the contracting parties, and a political league or alliance ; for any advance beyond
mere amity and mutual commerce, must amount
in some degree to that society in political objects
which constitutes the relation of allies.

But to form an alliance with the new people, is
virtually to acknowledge their independency ; and
that if we make this recognition, we ought at the
same time to engage them, if possible, in a defensive league against France, seems almost a political axiom. I shall, nevertheless, shew in the sequel,
the prudential necessity of this consequence. Meantime, as it is sufficiently obvious that my argument
is now reduced to a comparison between the third
and fourth of the projects proposed for discussion ;
and that recommendation of the one will, for the
most part, be an objection to the other, it may save
time, and prevent repetition, to consider them together.

The 3d and 4th Plans compared.

The same arguments which have been already
urged in favour of a commercial intercourse in general,

neral, and for giving that intercourse a conventional basis, will be found to recommend the going still further; for if we form commercial relations alone, the expected benefits will, in the first place, be less extensive, and in the second place, far less permanent, than they might be made by a political alliance.

1st. " They will be less extensive."

The beneficial effects to be expected from amity and commerce with the people of St. Domingo, are not only the acquisition of a valuable branch of trade, but a great diminution of the dangers to which Jamaica and our other sugar colonies will be in future exposed from the power of these formidable neighbours. Now both these advantages will be proportionate in their extent, to the degree in which agriculture shall be re-established and hereafter maintained in St. Domingo.

That this is true in respect of the commercial benefits, is sufficiently obvious; and it is fairly presumable, that as the mutual advantages of the intercourse shall increase, so also will the mutual amity and confidence which they naturally tend to inspire. The more amply these new customers are able to deal with us in the sale of their sugar and coffee, and in the purchase of our manufactures, the more they will find their comforts, their enjoyments, and growing prosperity, dependent upon English commerce; and the more carefully will they ob-

serve

serve that pacifie and amicable conduct towards our colonies, a violation of which would interrupt and diminish those blessings.

But some negative effects of their agricultural pursuits will be not less important to our future advantage and security ; for that military spirit which their late successes, and long exercise in war, must have strongly tended to inspire, will obviously be less general and less dangerous, in proportion as the cultivators are drawn back to their peaceful employments, and the rising generation trained, through the excitement of commerce, to the culture of the soil. The more of their youth they employ in the cane pieces, and the fewer they send to the drill, the less danger will there be that their indigenous military strength will soon be engaged in annoying their impotent neighbours.

But any great increase in agricultural industry, or abatement of military preparation, is not to be expected from them at this critical period, unless we determine to form with them more than commercial engagements.

There is now, let it be well considered, an object infinitely more interesting and important than agriculture or commerce to engage their anxious attention :—for after the dreadful experience they have had, they cannot safely conclude that the French government is even yet disposed to leave them in the undisturbed possession of their liberty.

The

The present maritime war gives them indeed a momentary security against invasion by the enemies of Great Britain; but if left to expect that upon the termination of our quarrel with the republic, they shall have again to struggle singly against that despotic and merciless power, against all the ruffians of France and all the bloodhounds of Cuba, not only for independence, but for freedom, and for life itself, the great and almost exclusive object of their present endeavours will naturally be to prepare the means of war.

In the contemplation of "*that horrible yoke which threatens them*," to use the words of the illustrious Toussaint, all minor considerations will be sunk. Instead of planting the sugar cane, the cotton bush, and the coffee tree, they will cultivate chiefly those provisions of which they may form plantations or lay up magazines in the interior, and thereby enlarge the means of subsistence in a new defensive war. Instead of rebuilding sugar mills and boiling houses, they will erect forts and cast up entrenchments. Instead of the manufactures of Birmingham or Manchester, they will import scarcely any thing but ammunition and arms. Of the rising generation, which we know from the best authority to be very numerous, the males, when of an age to be trained to labour, will be sent, not to the cane piece, but to the drill; and

G   a people

a people, on whose character the fate of the Antilles is suspended, will become a nation of soldiers.

Surely it is impossible that a British statesman, or a philanthropist, should contemplate this prospect without dismay. Not only will industry, order, civilization, and all the other blessings of social life, be retarded in their growth, but a national character formed in this new community, equally unfriendly to its own happiness, and tremendous to its European neighbours.

That St. Domingo, whatever course we take, will one day be mistress of the Western Archipelago, is indeed highly probable; and that the shocking slavery of our colonies cannot much longer be maintained, is sufficiently certain ; but by a just and rational policy, we might be enabled to look forward to the progress not only of African freedom, but of African sovereignty, in the West Indies, with satisfaction rather than dismay.

The subversion of establishments so guilty, and so fertile in misery and in death, both to Africa and Europe, can be deprecated only from the terrible nature of the means, by which the change, if sudden and hostile, must necessarily be effected, and the ruin in which it would involve individuals: and instead of a misfortune, it would be a great advantage, to this commercial and maritime empire, could we hereafter commute by compact

with

with an allied West Indian state, the costly and inconvenient sovereignty of those distant islands, for
a monopoly of their valuable trade. But if revolution, civil or political, should be introduced
into our sugar colonies by insurrection or hostile
force, dreadful indeed would be the effects to individuals, and pernicious to the nation at large.

Let it not then be considered as a question of
small moment, to what politicial character the *Indigenes*, as they call themselves, shall be at this critical period inclined. A restless warlike spirit in
them will soon carry liberty and African dominion
together in a tempest of revolution through all the
surrounding islands. On the contrary, a pacific
and industrious disposition in this infant society
would at least enable us to meet the approaching
change by timely preparation; and, perhaps, by the
spontaneous and gradual correction of existing
abuses, to introduce freedom generally into our colonies, the only mean of long preserving our sovereignty over them, without any disorder or mischief.
The happy effects of liberty and peace in St. Domingo would irresistibly influence the policy of all
European powers who possess colonies in the
West Indies, and incline them to a willing imita-
tion. Prejudice and self love might indeed still dispose the colonial party to oppose the salutary
change; but their influence, unhappily now too
powerful in this realm, would progressively de-
cline;

cline, falsehood would vanish before the clear light
of experience, the true interests of the nation
would be distinguished from the particular interests of the slave holder, and the chains of oppression would at length be loosened by the hand of
an impartial legislature.

What sedative then, Sir, can be found for that
warlike temper, so likely to mark the infancy of
this new community, and so much to be deprecated,
in a view both to commerce and security, except
the measures I propose ?

Tranquillize the minds of the new people on that
heart-stirring subject of anxiety, the defence of
their freedom, by guaranteeing it against the power
of France, and they will be enabled to reduce, instead of enlarging, their military establishment and
preparations; to restore the cultivators to the plantations, and to train up their youth to the peaceful
labours of the field. Relying upon the national
faith, and the maritime power of England, they
will feel no necessity for a larger internal force
than such a moderate army as may suffice to
maintain industry and order; they will, in a
word, revert to the wise policy of Toussaint,
and pursuing the maxims of that illustrious statesman and patriot, will apply themselves indefa-
tigably to the restitution of agriculture and commerce. You will reap the reward not only
in the rapid increase of a trade, to the mono
poly

poly of which you will acquire the strongest
of titles, but in the future security of Jamaica and
the rest of our valuable islands.

Here it may be proper to point out a new
and material difference between the present
circumstances of St. Domingo, and those which
existed there during our last war with France.
It was not so necessary in the former case, as
the present, to guard with anxiety against the
progress of a warlike character, and to encourage
carefully the restitution of peaceful industry;
because, after our pacification with Toussaint,
that general and his followers had no such powerful motives as must at present be felt by the African
leaders, for cherishing the one disposition, and
neglecting the other.

The black colonists, let it be remembered, had at
that time no apparent grounds of uneasiness in
regard to the intentions of the mother country
and naturally relied for the security of their free
dom, not only upon the assurances of the go
vernment, but upon the then unviolated law of the
republic, by which their title to all the rights of
French citizens was solemnly declared. It is
no impeachment of the discernment of Toussaint
to say, that he seems to have had no jealousy
on this momentous point; since even the interest of the republic, if rightly understood, would
have been a pledge for her good faith towards
                                        those

those loyal and useful citizens; and that the famous Buonaparte would be such a driveller as to act upon the prejudiced views of his wife's West Indian cabinet, and to imbibe their foolish antipathies to a black skin, at the expence not only of the colonial importance of France, but of his power of annoying this country, was an event too improbable to be believed antecedently to experience. It was not till after his preliminary treaty with England, that some broad indications of this extreme folly for the first time appeared in his public language and conduct.

Certain however it is, that the African chief was deceived; and down to the moment of Leclerc's invasion, reposed with implicit confidence on the treacherous assurances of the government. Hence that great man felt himself at liberty, after his convention with General Maitland, to indulge freely his beneficent wishes for the restitution of agriculture and commerce. His army was chiefly employed in the support of a police framed to promote these pacific objects, and it is demonstrable from the French official accounts, that a great part of his military followers must have been restored to their agricultural employments: for his enemies had more temptation to exaggerate than to diminish his force; and yet Leclerc's dispatches described the regular black troops as amounting only to a few thousands

and

and the cultivators, who quitted their plantations
in order to flock to the standard of Toussaint, as
composing the bulk, not only of the general population, but of the army by which the cause of
freedom was sustained.

We cannot expect that the successors of this
hero, unless furnished with better security than
that upon which he fatally relied, will pursue,
at the present period, the same course of policy.
No professions, and no practical measures of the
French government, can renew in their minds
the confidence which had so dreadful an issue.
As Toussaint was fatally in haste to sink the
warrior in the legislator, the new leaders will, if
left to their own resources, take an opposite
course. He was at once the Romulus, and
the Numa, of St. Domingo, but Dessalines will
be rather the Hostilius.

Nothing, in short, but the security which their
dear bought freedom might derive by being placed
under the safeguard of Great Britain, can prevent
this new people from devoting all their resources
to preparations for future war; from neglecting those arts which might render them most
valuable friends to us, and cultivating those habits
which will make them most formidable neighbours.

I remarked, in the second place, that the advantages, commercial and political, of a trade with
St

St. Domingo, would, without the proposed alliance, " be less permanent" than such an alliance might make them.

The negro chiefs will probably be willing enough to enter with us into a treaty simply commercial, should they find that no more can be obtained; or even without a treaty, they will allow us freely to trade to their ports; and under the circumstances of the moment, amicable conduct towards the subjects of this country will perhaps be carefully observed ; but if we wish for a lasting privilege or preference beyond other foreigners, we must, as already observed, obtain it by compact; and though we are the only people on earth who dare at this moment to accept of such a grant, yet in order effectually to obtain and preserve it, we must give in return some equivalent benefit.

The reciprocity of commercial advantage alone will not entitle us for a moment to any such distinction ; for in this respect other nations will have equal or superior pretensions. Their vessels will bring the commodities of Europe and America into the ports of St. Domingo for sale upon terms at least as cheap as those of the British importer; and will receive West India produce in return, at a price at least as high as our merchants can afford to offer. In order, therefore, to outbid all other competitors, we must add to mere mercantile considerations,

what

what we alone can offer, and entitle ourselves not only to a present predilection, but future gratitude and attachment, by the offer of a defensive alliance.

Should it be supposed, that the assistance which has, for our own sakes, and in a very equivocal spirit, been given towards the expulsion of a common enemy, would at the present moment be so favourably considered, as to procure for us, without any further consideration, a commercial preference to other nations, the permanence of any advantages which should upon that account alone be obtained, might still be reasonably doubted. The powerful motive of self-interest would be wanting to ensure their stability; they would soon therefore be viewed with a grudging eye, as the price of services which were past, and the value whereof had perhaps been over-rated: rival merchants would represent our privileges as unreasonable restraints of trade, and labour, not without success, to render them unpopular in the island, till they might at length become, rather sources of contention, than bonds of mutual amity.

Not so, if a great or exclusive preference of British commerce, were the stipulated consideration for a guarantee of their freedom and a perpetual defensive alliance. In that case, our privileges would stand upon the strongest and most durable

H   pillars

pillars that the gratitude and self-love of the new people, could conjointly raise to support them; the British flag would be regarded as the palladium of their social happiness and safety, and an attachment might be expected to ensue, not less powerful and lasting than their love of liberty, or their antipathy to a horrible bondage.

So assiduous and successful have been the arts of calumny against this much injured race, that with those who have viewed them only in the pictures drawn by their oppressors, it may not be here unnecessary to assert their claim to human character in the sense of benefits conferred *. National gratitude is certainly a virtue which the page of history does not often exhibit in the conduct of polished societies; but if any one doubts whether the people of St. Domingo can distinguish and

* See a shocking instance of misrepresentation on this head in an author of no vulgar name, well exposed by Mr. Brougham in his able work on the Colonial Policy of the European Powers, vol. ii. p. 458.

This work, though it contains some important errors, abounds in valuable information, deep reflection, and ingemous argument upon West Indian affairs. Mr. B.'s views of practical policy in relation to St. Domingo were diametrically opposite to those which were developed in the Crisis, and which it is the object of these sheets to impress; but Mr. B. wrote when, in common with the European public in general, he thought a counter revolution in that island an attainable object. The contrary being now demonstrated, the author may safely invoke much of that gentleman's reasoning as auxiliary to his own.

adhere

adhere to their public benefactors, let him advert to their unprecedented steadiness of attachment to all their faithful leaders. From the first establishment of their freedom, till they were treacherously bereaved of Toussaint, their fidelity to that great man, in peace, as well as war, was truly remarkable; and since his fall, Dessalines and Christophe, who were his most faithful adherents, and principal officers, have been objects of as steady an attachment. I rely, however, upon principles much surer and stronger than gratitude, which would bind them for ever to Great Britain, should she now become the patroness and guardian of their freedom.

We have hitherto adverted only to those commercial benefits, and that better security of our sugar colonies from revolutionary dangers, which might be derived from the proposed alliance. But the same measure is necessary to avert some political inconveniences and perils of a more direct and comprehensive kind, which are likely to flow from the present state of St. Domingo. These I will proceed to consider,

1st. As they belong to the existing state of affairs.

2d. As they will arise in future, but certain, or highly probable situations.

At this moment, the various political relations of St. Domingo are singular, and highly perplexing.

The

[52]

The new state is at war with all our confederated enemies, and at war also with one of our friends. It is the foe of France and Holland, who are also our foes, and yet is not our confederate; it is equally hostile to Spain with whom we are in amity, and yet is at peace with ourselves.

What makes these cross relations more singular and more embarrassing, is, that the principal parties to them are all placed within sight of each others territories. The same visible horizon comprises, together with St. Domingo, some of the most important colonial coasts of Spain and Great Britain; and for all the purposes of war against the negro people, Cuba, which is one of those neighbouring shores, may be regarded as a colony of France. It is from the ports on the East end of that island, and from that station alone, that the French cruizers and fugitive troops are now feebly annoying their sable enemies, and menacing them with a new descent.

A man must be totally ignorant of the navigation and trade of the gulph of Mexico, not to perceive at a single glance the mischievous tendency of this state of things to the commerce of Great Britain, and the disputes which it must soon unavoidably occasion between such of the parties as are yet at peace with each other.

Let us advert, for instance, to that profitable trade which is carried on between our free ports

in

in the West Indies, and the Spanish colonies. A great part of the goods which are the subject of that commerce, are, during their transit to and from our ports, the property of Spaniards, and of course liable to capture and condemnation by these sable enemies of Spain, the only foes she now has to seize them; and though no inconsiderable portion of the same lucrative trade is carried on upon account of our own merchants, yet from the rigid system of the cabinet of Madrid, the British owner is for the most part obliged to cover his property under the names of Spaniards, and to send it in vessels really or ostensibly Spanish. The consequence is, that when vessels engaged in this trade shall be captured by the cruizers of St. Domingo, they and their cargoes, though actually British, will be apparently hostile.

Such property will, by the law of nations, be fairly confiscable, even though the fact of British ownership should be capable of being clearly established; for it is a principle in the prize court, that a hostile flag and papers are conclusive against the claimant. But supposing the negro chiefs to be either uninformed of this law, or so indulgent towards our merchants as to wave its application, and allow them, on proof of their property in such cases, to obtain restitution; still very serious expence, inconvenience, and loss, must be sustained before their claims could be established: nor is it

easy

easy to say what species of evidence would or ought to satisfy the captors, or a prize tribunal, that property embarked in a transaction wholly conducted by enemies, and avowed by all the papers to be hostile, really belongs to a friend. That such captures would at least be a fertile source of troublesome and dangerous disputes, is certain; nor can it be doubted that they would very greatly discourage, if not wholly ruin, a trade highly beneficial to this country.

The effects of these hostilities between St. Domingo and Cuba, will be the more vexatious, because by them only, at this period, can the peace of the Gulph of Mexico and of the Windward Passage be disturbed. We shall lose through this cause alone, the profound tranquillity which our commerce might otherwise, from circumstances unprecedented in any former war, enjoy in that part of the world. Though France has now no port to leeward of Guadaloupe, though St. Domingo is amicable to us, and Spain is still indulged with the rights of neutrality, yet British property may be captured, and British navigation greatly disturbed, in that important gulph, and its outlets, even within sight of Jamaica.

Whether any great inconveniences have hitherto arisen from this situation of things, I am not informed. In some degree its bad effects doubtless

have

have already been felt; but the surrender of the
Cape, and the expulsion of the French from St.
Domingo, were, at the date of the last advices
from that quarter which have been given to the
public, very recent events; and the hostilities
between that island and Cuba had but just commenced. Their noxious tendency therefore in re-
regard to British commerce, could not well so soon
have displayed itself, in any very extensive consequences.

These hostilities, however, will, in all probability, soon be greatly increased both in their extent
and activity. The *Indigenes*, otherwise called, like
all the other brave opposers of French usurpation,
Brigands, were able, even during their arduous
contest with Rochambeau, to fit out many armed
boats and vessels, which greatly annoyed the commerce of their enemies on various parts of the
coast; but now, when the harbours are in their
possession, and when they have no enemy in the
interior, their cruizers will naturally become far
more numerous; and many of them will probably
be of sufficient force to attack openly the largest
merchant-men, if not also any armed vessels, by
which they are likely to be opposed. Within a
short distance of their shores, or in either of those
narrow but important channels which divide them
from Cuba and Jamaica, it will soon not be easy to
navigate without encountering that yet new and
undescribed

undescribed phenomenon, the flag of the West Indian republic.

Is it asked by what means this rude community will be able speedily to acquire ships and naval stores? Every capture which they make will add to their petty marine such a bottom as may be fit for annoying, in those calm seas, the unarmed merchantmen of their enemy, many of which are continually passing within sight of their ports: nor can it be doubted that they have even at the present moment, produce enough to barter with neutral merchants for such naval and military stores as may suffice for the equipment of their vessels. Indeed the valuable cargoes which must fall into their hands, will soon furnish an ample fund to pay for these, and all other necessary supplies.

But privateering, let me add, is a species of trade which will never be at a stand through the want of capital, where there is a good prospect of profitable captures; and if the proper resources of the new state itself should be inadequate to the fitting out of a sufficient number of cruizers effectually to annoy their enemies, they will be at no loss for foreign assistance, not even, strange though it may seem, for that of his Majesty's subjects. The rich commerce of the Spanish West Indies is a bait which always fascinates the eyes of our seamen, and of all adventurers, accus

tomed

tomed to engage in the business of privateering, especially such of them as inhabit or frequent the Bahama and Bermuda islands; and these men now regard with impatience the delay of a war with Spain; for as to the trade of the few colonies remaining to France and Holland, it offers to such sportsmen but poor game any where; and in the Gulph of Mexico, or its passages, scarcely any at all. Rely upon it, therefore, that should we much longer continue at peace with the court of Madrid, no small part of the privateering capital and enterprize of British subjects will be transferred from our own colomes to St. Domingo. At the same time, the remnant of the old Buccaneer race still remaining dispersed in various parts of the West Indies, and who assume always that particular national character which favours most for the moment their love of contraband employment and maritime plunder, will flock with avidity to the ports of that island, to engage under the new flag in their accustomed pursuits.

Never since Hispaniola was rendered formidable by the exploits of that piratical race, not even when, during the 17th century, they revelled at once in the spoils both of Spanish and English commerce, were there such dazzling inducements offered to privateers-men, as the same island at the present conjuncture holds forth. Not only will the trade of Porto Rico, the rich com-

I   merce

merce of the Havannah, and the great exports
of Cuba at large, increased as they are of late
years far beyond all former example, be a sure
and easy prey, but a great part also of the trea-
sures of Mexico and Peru may be intercepted on
its passage to Europe by the cruizers of this
centrical island: and the facility of bringing the
spoil into port, will be not less tempting, than the
ease with which it can be captured.

Let the possible effects of these combinations
be pursued by the eye of state prudence beyond the present day. I have already adverted
to the consequences of a military spirit being
formed in this infant society; but would an ap-
petence for maritime capture, be less dangerous
to their commercial neighbours? Their war with
the Spanish colonies may sow deep in this new
soil the seeds of a predatory disposition, which,
springing up among the first shoots of social
habits and institutions, may be found very hard
to eradicate, and the independent Africans of
the Antilles, may hereafter, like those of Barbary,
be a scourge to all maritime powers.

Should it be objected to these calculations, that
Spain, not having acknowledged the independency of St. Domingo, and being at peace with
France, might reasonably treat the negro priva-
teersmen and their foreign associates as pirates;
I answer, that it would argue great ignorance of
the character of such adventurers, and of the
spirit

spirit of privateering in general, to suppose that
such severity would materially check their career.
It would be much easier indeed for Spain to threat-
en such penalties, than actually to inflict them;
for so slender is her maritime force in the West
Indies, when compared with the extent of her
possessions and trade in that quarter, that she cannot check, in any tolerable degree, that enormous
contraband commerce with her colonies, which
notoriously prevails. Although her guarda costa's
are sufficiently disposed to make seizures, the
smuggler despises their feeble efforts, and carries
on, often by day light, and upon the very coasts
they are appointed to guard, a trade, which, in
case of capture, would consign him to slavery for
life. With how much more facility would the
hostile cruizers of St. Domingo be able, on the
open seas or near their own shores, to elude the
few armed ships of Spain, from which her scat-
tered commerce might occasionally derive protection; and how inadequate would such slight
danger of capture be, to repress the ardent spirit
of privateering! So easy is it on those extensive
and accessible coasts to escape into port, that the
brigand boats, as they were called, frequently
captured the merchantmen which brought supplies to Rochambeau, even while a strong French
squadron was stationed at the Cape, and while
the principal harbours were still in possession
of their enemy. Need it be added, that the consequence

quence of their being made prisoners by the French at that time, would have been death to these enterprizing men, and death too in some horrible form? The Spaniards, however, will scarcely dare to treat as pirates, men acting under the commission of a government which is *de facto* independent, and which is well able to practise a dreadful retaliation.

Without dwelling longer on this copious subject, I may safely consider it as proved, that if the harvest of Spanish booty is to be reaped by the cruizers of St. Domingo, and by them only, there will be no want of labourers or sickles for the work.

" But would such a treaty as is proposed be a preventative of all the evils, commercial and political, to which we have adverted?" It would give us, I answer, the best attainable security against them.

Such an alliance with the negro chiefs would, for instance, intitle us in so high a degree to their confidence and favour, that a pass from our government might be allowed by them to operate as a sufficient protection to British property, even when found in the hands of enemies, and under a Spanish disguise. They would probably go still further, and allow Spanish vessels to pass unmolested to and from British ports, even when trading on their own account. At all events, a full persuasion of our sincere amity in the breast

of

of the new government, would be a safeguard against dangerous contentions; and would insure to us easy redress, when our commerce might, through the ignorance or misconduct of individuals, be improperly disturbed.

Our great influence might, however, extend to purposes still more beneficial and important. We might very possibly engage our grateful allies to renounce their just enmity towards the Spaniards; and thus, with the concurrence of the latter, completely restore peace to those seas, in the tranquillity of which we have so large an interest. It would be no unequal condition in the proposed league, to require, as a consideration of the important guarantee we should give, that our new allies should be hereafter the friend of our friends, as well as the enemy of our enemies; and as to Spain, she would have little right or inclination to complain, should we, in consequence of such an alliance, demand of her the termination of a war, which, without any rational object on her part, must be a present nuisance to her colonies as well as our own, and threatens to both in its progress the most pernicious and destructive effects.

The court of Madrid must, doubtless, already view with regret a troublesome and useless quarrel, in which nothing but necessary complaisance to the French republic, could have induced it to engage; and would rejoice to procure a peace through our mediation, if without violence to the

same

same necessary principle, that end could be attained.

I presume not indeed to say whether France would permit such a measure—I cannot venture to conjecture how long the neutrality of Spain may be deemed by the consul more important to his treasury, than her co-operation in the war would be to his arms; nor, on the other hand, can I presume to appreciate those considerations, by which our own court has been induced to treat hitherto, and may be led still to treat, as a friend, this tributary vassal of France. But as Buonaparte must have powerful reasons for permitting so dependent and obsequious a neighbour to preserve her pacific attitude, and to admit freely into her ports that odious British commerce which he is anxious to banish from the Continent, the same motives may perhaps induce him to relinquish the object of giving to his sable enemies a trivial annoyance from the ports of Cuba, should he find that a neutrality towards them is firmly demanded from the Spanish court by the ministers of this country.

If, on the contrary, a measure essential to the safe passage of the colonial wealth of Spain in its way to Europe, and consequently to the French exchequer, should be prohibited by the consul, it might perhaps deserve to be well considered, whether his latent views in such conduct must not be of a kind highly dangerous to this country; and

whether

whether the disadvantages of our amity with Spain
in the West Indies, were not in that case greater
than the balance of precarious profit which we
derive from it in Europe. Let it be recollected,
that her war with St. Domingo is the only pretence upon which that power could compatibly
with the general laws of neutrality towards this
country, allow--French ships of war to be fitted
out, and rendezvous in the ports of Cuba; and at
the same time let an estimate be made of the annoyance to which our commerce must inevitably
be exposed through this permission, and of the
additional waste of men and money to which we
shall in consequence be subjected on the Jamaica
station. Remove this nuisance by removing the
pretext for it, and France will not have a port
to leeward of Guadaloupe from which she can fit
out a single privateer.

But if, in the case last considered, it should be
thought more prudent to submit to some of the
inconveniences which have been suggested, than
to obviate them at the expence of a rupture with
Spain ; still a strict amity and alliance with the
negro chiefs, would avert from us a great part of
the impending evils. If we could not restore
peace to the Gulph of Mexico, and its outlets, at
least we should obtain the best chance of preserving our pacific and commercial relations with
both the neighbouring combatants, and that with
the least possible degree of inconvenience and loss.

Having

Haviug thus far adverted to the inconveniences
and dangers, which, during our existing political
relations, are likely to spring from the new state
of St. Domingo, let us next, as was proposed,
consider those which are likely to flow from the
same source, in future, but certain or highly probable situations.

If we anticipate, in the first place, an event,
which must be admitted to be highly probable, that
of Spain becoming a party to the present war, as
our enemy, and the confederate of France, it will
be found, that the same causes which have already
been stated, would still operate very unfavourably
to our commerce, as well as to our colonial security.

It was the policy of our government, during the
last war, to profit by the necessities of the Spanish
colonies, so as to supply them, notwithstanding the
existing hostilities, with our manufactures, in ex-
change for their produce and bullion ; and though all
commerce with an enemy is in general prohibited,
under penalty of confiscation of the property engaged in it, yet in favour of this particular branch
of trade, that rule of the law of war was dispensed
with by orders of his Majesty in council *. British
subjects were permitted to trade upon their own
account to and from the ports of Spanish America ; and the subjects of Spain were protected by

* Orders of Council of 28th March, 1st May, and 7th Au-
gust, 1798.

the

the same authority, in trading as in time of peace to our free ports in the West Indies. Licences from our governors exempted the vessels and cargoes engaged in such commerce from capture; or in case of their being seized, intitled the British or Spanish owners to immediate restitution.

From the same important national considerations upon which this indulgence was founded, we may reasonably expect its renewal, in the event of a new quarrel with Spain; and beyond doubt, our manufacturers and merchants are greatly interested in the maintenance of such commercial policy in that quarter of the globe.

But here the hostilities between the Spanish colonies and St. Domingo, will present to us new and most formidable obstacles; for in war, as well as in peace, our trade with those colonies has always, by their own law, been strictly prohibited; and could only be carried on clandestinely, by means of fictitious papers, under the Spanish flag, and a tually, or ostensibly, on account of merchants of that.nation. Even during the greatest straits to which their colonies were reduced by our hostilities in the late war, through the dearth of essential supplies, their vessels were seized and confiscated by their own government, when detected in trading to or from a British port. It is obvious, therefore, that the property which may be engaged in this trade during a future war with Spain, will be ex-

K   posed

posed to the same jeopardy, and be subject to the same inconveniencies and losses, that have already been pointed out, in respect of our now subsisting intercourse with those colonies.

We shall obviously have no right to protect the ships or goods of Spanish merchants from the hostilities of their new enemy, though we may exempt them from our own; and to elicit the fact of British ownership from the mass of Spanish evidences in which it is disguised, would, as before observed, be a very difficult or impracticable task. A trade, therefore, which already not only exposes the property embarked in it, but the persons of the immediate agents, to serious dangers, would be subjected to such new and formidable additional risques, that it must be greatly discouraged and diminished, if not wholly destroyed.

The operations of war carried on from the neighbouring coasts of Jamaica and St. Domingo against an enemy within sight of both, could not fail to produce other, and numerous, occasions of dispute, and of serious public inconvenience, unless the mutual stipulations of a treaty, and the good will and confidence arising from an express confederacy, were the wholesome expedients of prevention.

Cases of joint capture, for instance, and of recapture or rescue, would in those narrow channels very frequently occur; and the necessary but

invidious

invidious right of search, must be exercised on both sides, between the independent and unallied belligerents. The neutral ships trading to the ports of St. Domingo, and their cargoes, would also be subjects of frequent and dangerous controversy; especially as the new people will have occasion largely to import articles of a contraband nature, and as the pretence of a destination to their ports, might be made a specious mask for the conveyance of such noxious goods to Cuba, or to the Spanish main. Questions of still greater delicacy and danger might arise, from the opposite principles which would be applied by our captors, and those of the new state respectively, to the natives of Africa, or creole negroes, found on board prize vessels; especially should they be the subject of joint capture, or of recapture; or should they, by any other means, be supposed to be privileged by the new sanctuary of African captives and bondsmen.

And here another copious source of discord presents itself. To what extent shall the harbours and roadsteads of St. Domingo on the one side, and of Jamaica on the other, be privileged from the operations of war against any cruizers but their own? or how far shall the property of prizes made within their limits, vest in the government of the country to which they belong?

Without anticipating any further grounds of
controversy,

controversy, I may safely affirm, that the most anxious conventional precautions, and that confidence which belongs to the most unequivocal amity, can alone secure us, in the case last supposed, from pernicious and fatal disputes; and that whatever chance we may have of avoiding, under present circumstances, a quarrel with the people of St. Domingo, their speedy enmity would, unless prevented by an alliance, be almost an inevitable consequence of hostilities between this country and Spain.

It may, perhaps, at first sight be thought that hatred to a common enemy, would be a sufficient bond of attachment; and that when at war with the only hostile neighbour of the new state, we should have influence enough over this inferior co-belligerent for every useful purpose, without any express alliance. But as there would be no common cause, or mutual object in the war, much less any claim on our part to be considered as volunteer auxiliaries, the negro chiefs could feel little disposition to abate for our sakes any part of their belligerent rights; much less to conduct their war upon principles calculated to consult our convenience, interest, or security, at the expence of their own.

It would not be forgotten by them, that Spain had been suffered to lend the ports of Cuba to the French fugitives, for purposes hostile to St. Domingo;

St. Domingo; and that the measure, though dangerous to ourselves, had not been regarded by us as any violation of her neutrality to this country, merely because the Indigenes were the immediate objects of annoyance. Perhaps the memory of these chiefs might take a still longer retrospect, and by suggesting to them our conduct towards the illustrious Toussaint, at the conclusion of our former war with France, might admonish them to look in the existing contest to their own security alone; lest by furthering our selfish views, they should only accelerate a new invasion, and a new surprise, by the armies of the republic. The extraordinary measure of our destroying or carrying away their means of defence upon the surrender to our ships of certain fortresses, after those places had been previously reduced, at the expence of much African blood, to the necessity of an immediate capitulation, might also be remembered; and, to be sure, no conduct could indicate more plainly a design on our part of resuming towards them our former policy, on the close of our new quarrel with France.

But such indications of a separate and selfish object in our war with their enemies, would not be necessary to teach them to take care of themselves. It would be enough that we had not acknowledged their independency, much less undertaken to defend it; and that there was no

conventional

conventional association with them in those hostilities in which we had, at length, for our own
sakes, engaged. In the selfish and discordant pro-
pensities of human nature, at least, the calumniators of the African race will not refuse them a
share; and their friends, on the other hand, will
neither admit them to be so dull, nor assert that
they are so preposterously generous, as to renounce,
for the sake of our constrained co-operation, the
care of their own interest and safety. For my
part, I should expect as little regard from them
to their reluctant foreign coadjutors, as if they
had been educated at Vienna or Berlin; and should
look for as little of practical concert, and mutual
deference, between the casual co-belligerents of
the Antilles, as was exhibited between those of
the late war in Europe.

In the case immediately under consideration,
and in all our future wars, much of positive advantage would be lost, as well as very serious
evils incurred, should you neglect to avail yourself, as I advise, of the present happy opportunity.

The geographical position of St. Domingo is
such, as would make the free use of its ports, of
the greatest importance to either party in a war
between this country and its ancient enemies.
From no station can the trade of Cuba and the
Mexican provinces be so effectually annoyed; and
that

that it completely locks in and commands the island of Jamaica, an inspection of the map, with attention to the course of the trade wind, will sufficiently demonstrate.

The importance of the island in a maritime war has hitherto been infinitely less than it is likely in future to prove ; because, since the colonial interests, and the naval strength of Great Britain and France fully attained to their great and long continued preponderance, and engaged those leading powers in frequent West Indian wars, St. Domingo and the Spanish colonies have never till now been hostile to each other, but have been under the dominion of allied and confederated sovereigns. The belligerent consequence of this great island, therefore, has been chiefly felt in the annoyance given by French ships, rendezvousing in its ports, to the commerce of Jamaica; and this effect has been mitigated, not only by the great naval force of this country, which has enabled us to keep up strong squadrons on that station, and to employ very powerful convoys, but from the immense extent and value of the exports of St. Domingo itself, and of the Spanish colonies, which obliged our allied enemies for the most part to limit their maritime efforts in that quarter to purposes merely defensive. Many of our merchantmen from Jamaica, indeed, were carried into the ports of St. Domingo, but a much larger proportion of

the

the enemy's ships which sailed to and from those ports, were captured by British cruizers; so that the balance of prize acquisition and loss, was usually much in our favour. It may be added, that great incidental protection was afforded to our commerce in the windward passage, and the Gulph, by the numerous British privateers which, invited by the hope of falling in with rich St. Domingo-men, made those seas their constant resort.

A moment's attention to the singular reverse in most of these circumstances which must arise from the great change that has lately taken place, will suffice to shew the important influence which the amity or enmity of the new state, would have upon our maritime interests, in our wars with our ancient enemies.

Hispaniola, no longer under the dominion of the house of Bourbon, or of that power, styling itself a republic, which has seized upon one of the thrones of the Bourbons, will, if hostile to Spain, and in confederacy with ourselves, be found a most important ally. With the numerous ports on the North, South, and West of this large island at our command, and with an auxiliary army of negroes at our call, our power to distress the Spanish colonies and commerce, would be as wide as our inclination to do so. From the same advantages, the defence of Jamaica, and of all our commerce in the Gulph of Mexico, would

would be a work of unprecedented cheapness and facility.

Great on the other hand, beyond all former experience, would be the annoyance to which we should be exposed by the hostility of St. Domingo, supposing its government to side in future wars with a maritime enemy of this country. While Jamaica, perpetually menaced with invasion by a negro army, would cost us a frightful waste of British lives, as well as treasure, in a service merely defensive, our trade in that quarter would be harassed by the undiverted operations of such ships and squadrons, as a European enemy, the ally of the new state, might send to rendezvous in its harbours. Nor would these evils be compensated in any material degree by such rich spoils as were formerly made from the commerce of St. Domingo ; for supposing its exports to regain even their former magnitude, the new political relations of the island would rescue them from the grasp of our cruizers. Its external commerce, to whatever extent revived, would no longer be conducted on account of the islanders themselves, or of our European enemies, but being at all times entirely in the hands of foreign merchants, would in time of war, be carried on upon account of such foreigners only as should possess the advantage of neutral character ; the property engaged

L   in

in it would consequently, unless under special circumstances, be exempt from capture. That important belligerent right, the right of maintaining against neutral intervention in time of war, the commercial restrictions by which a hostile government had monopolized the trade of its colonies in time of peace, will here have no application. In this, and many other respects, we shall experience the important difference between a trans-atlantic enemy, the satellite of some European power; and the same enemy, when enfranchised from all exterior connection, and acting against us as a principal in the war, or an independent confederate.

To undervalue or slight these considerations on account of the present depression of the French marine, and the pacific disposition of Spain, or because France has no longer any territory in the Leeward division of the Antilles, would be highly improvident ; for of these extenuatory circumstances, the two latter may be very speedily reversed, and the first considerably altered. The Consul could, no doubt, with a single mandate, obtain the cession of Porto Rico, or even Cuba, as well as compel the court of Madrid to join him in the war; and that the navy of France may be one day sufficiently restored to be troublesome to our commerce and colonies, is surely no impossible event.

Whether

Whether then, sir, you regard the probable effects in the West Indies of our existing relations, or anticipate the changes likely to take place in those relations before we can sheath the sword, or look forward, with a providence which the state of Europe loudly demands, to future wars, the prudence of embracing the present fortunate opportunity is too manifest to be denied. In either view, it is of vast importance to insure, if possible, that the new born West Indian power shall hereafter be propitious to ourselves, and adverse to our enemies.

But to this end no half measures will suffice. If a connection merely commercial will not, as has been already shown, be an adequate security against discord and future enmity, much less will it entitle us to the positive benefits, which we might derive from more intimate relations with the new people, when at war with a maritime power. A commercial treaty might indeed so far abate their reasonable distrust, that they might no longer fear to admit our ships of war into their harbours, as Dessalines apparently did, when he declined to furnish us with pilots * ; but if we would have the

free

* At the Cape. See Gazette of February 7th, 1804. It is a pity that the whole correspondence upon the subject of the capitulation with Rochambeau was not published, because the apparent mutilation

free use of their ports for the purposes of naval equipment and enterprize, and avail ourselves in other respects of their very important aid against a common enemy, as well as guard against their great power of future annoyance, we must conciliate their confidence and attachment, by a defensive alliance

Were I to stop here, considerations enough perhaps have been offered in support of the plan recommended to justify its immediate adoption, unless more weighty objections than I am able to anticipate can be placed in the opposite scale.

But these, cogent though they appear to be, are by no means the most important or urgent, of the motives that call for such a measure.

The grand, and I will venture to add, the conclusive, arguments yet remain to be opened.

———

Hitherto we have not supposed the possibility of a speedy reconciliation between St. Domingo and France—nor have we considered the conse-

mutilation of it, leaves room for conjecture, that the negro chief had still better grounds for his conduct than met the public eye. Was it intended to destroy or carry away the military stores at the Cape, as well as at Fort Dauphin ? A refusal of Rochambeau to permit us so far to frustrate his capitulation with Dessalines, or at least his refusal to capitulate to our squadron on those terms, would appear to have been one cause of the resentment which his conduct inspired at Jamaica.

quences

quences of leaving the republic on the termination of the present war, in possession of her
claim to that island—but to these most momentous and alarming views of our subject, I must
now proceed to invite your serious attention.

And first, let us advert to the chance of a reconciliation, between the Indigenes and their former
masters.

If wrongs the most perfidious, cruel, and exas-
perating, that were ever offered by a government
to a people, could to a certainty preclude the
chance of future amity between them, St. Domingo must be for ever lost to France, not only as a
province, but a friend. It seems at this moment a
monstrous notion even, and injurious to the character of the brave Indigenes, to conceive that
they can ever be brought again to profess themselves, subjects or friends of the republic. Their
unparalleled wrongs appear to justify, and even to
demand from them, an indignation against their
barbarous oppressors never to be ended or as-
suaged.

" Immortale odium, et nunquam sanabile vulnus."

But let us not draw precipitate conclusions
upon this truly important subject.

That the present despot of France should ever
again conciliate the confidence of that injured
people,

people, is indeed I hope impossible. He has pro
bably sinned against them beyond forgiveness,
and has deceived and betrayed them so basely,
as to preclude all future faith in his promises
or his oaths.—But Buonaparte, let it be remembered, is not immortal; nor is his authority, secure from a sudden and speedy subversion.

What changes the death or deposition of that
tyrant might make in the European policy of
France, it is not easy to foresee; but this may
with almost certainty be predicted, that in what
regards her West India colonies, his measures
would be totally reversed. The loss of St. Domingo, the new infamy brought upon the French
name by his detestable conduct in the Antilles,
the sacrifice of sixty thousand brave and veteran
troops by a project which both in its conception
and its intemperate prosecution, was superlatively
wicked and weak—these are faults which his inimical successors would be happy to blazon, and which
even a new government friendly to his memory,
could such a one be expected to succeed to his
power, would find it more politic to exhibit than
conceal.

Those pernicious measures had, prior even to
their ignominious catastrophe, become very unpopular; especially with the army; and it may be
questioned whether they were not so from the
beginning,

beginning, with a great majority of the people of France. But now at least, their fatal effects must be a source of general discontent; and would furnish reason enough to a new administration, for condemning the past, and adopting an opposite system.

How powerfully must these considerations be strengthened by recent events! — A new war with England, the reconquest of some of the Windward Islands, the danger of the rest, and the ultimate evacuation of St. Domingo, have brought back a state of things such as led the convention, in 1794, to decree enfranchisement to the colonial negroes at large; and such as must make even the Consul himself deplore his own egregious folly, in wholly reversing that decree. If not yet heartily inclined to retrace his steps, and to replace on the side of France, allies who could not only make for him a most powerful diversion of the regular British army, but enable him to preserve his remaining colonies, and to stab deep into the bosom of our commerce, it must be because his despotic pride, and the influence of his West Indian connections united, are an overmatch for his policy, and even for his hatred of England. But his successors, on whom such a reverse of system would reflect no disgrace, would infallibly be disposed to adopt it; at least in respect of St. Domingo.

They

They would first, probably attempt to regain the sovereignty of the island ; by offering such a solemn recognition of freedom, and such security for its future maintenance, as might induce the Indigenes to wave their claim of independency, and again to profess themselves citizens of the Republic. But supposing this attempt to fail, political independency, would probably be conceded. upon the condition of their giving to France the exclusive right of trading to their ports, and entering with her into a perpetual alliance. If the new governors of the Republic should be enlightened politicians, they may possibly perceive that such a confederacy would make St. Domingo far more valuable to France, and more formidable to England, than it would become even by the renewal of its former subjection.

Upon such a basis as this, the practicability of a reconciliation cannot reasonably be doubted. But that a submission even to the sovereignty of the Republic, would be inexorably refused to a government, by which the odious power of the Consul had been overthrown, is by no means certain.

The new rulers of France would be able speciously, and even truly, to ascribe to the despotic government which they had abolished, those hideous sins against the African race, by which the Republic had been disgraced ; and credibly to alledge

ledge that the trans atlantic measures of the Con
sul had been as opposite to the sense of the
French people, as to the dictates of justice and
humanity. At the time, it might be said, when
the freedom of the colonial negroes was perfidiously invaded, that of the French citizens in
Europe had been totally suppressed; and a new
reign of terror, had made them irresponsible for
the acts of the second Robertspierre.

In justice to our unhappy enemies, it must be
acknowledged, that they have in this case as fair
an apology, as their own enslaved condition can
afford. It is a striking fact, that the law brought
into the senate by the agents of the Consul, to
revive the slave trade, and abrogate that charter
of colonial freedom, the decree of February, 1794,
was opposed with much greater boldness, than any
of those domestic innovations by which that assembly was made to sacrifice its own boasted rights, and
the liberty of the Republic. No less than twenty-
seven members had the courage and the virtue to
vote against that execrable law, in opposition to
a government majority of fifty-four *. In an attempt to conciliate the negroes of St. Domingo,
this fact would not be forgotten, and might fairly
produce a very considerable effect.

* Paris Newspapers of May 20th, 1802.

M   It

It is obvious, that if such apologies for past conduct, should suffice to appease the resentment, and remove the suspicion of the black colonists, or if a new French government should prudently limit its pretensions to a mode of connection of which confidence is no indispensible basis, there are many powerful inducements which would dispose the new people to intimate connections with France, in preference to any other nation.

Unity of language is one of these motives, of which among an illiterate people, the effect will be peculiarly great.

But a still more powerful sympathy will be found in the unity of religious worship, and tenets.

The slaves in the French islands, prior to the revolution, were by no means wholly neglected in point of religious culture. Many pious missionaries, laboured earnestly for their instruction and conversion, and were protected and aided by the government, in the prosecution of that charitable work. Nor did the established clergy of those islands, regard this degraded class as unworthy of their pastoral care : so that by the concurrence of regular and irregular efforts, a large proportion of the negroes, were brought to as much knowledge of Christianity, as is usually the portion of the poor and

illiterate

illiterate in the Roman Catholic countries of Europe. Masters, or colonial assemblies, were not left at liberty, *as in some other colonies*, to gratify their own latent infidelity, or their prejudices against the African race, by obstructing either the parish priests or missionaries, in this part of their clerical duty.

Religion brought in her train, to these unhappy men, temporal, as well as spiritual comforts. They obtained, during the great annual festivals of the church, periods of repose which the master durst not invade ; and found in their confessor, one of the awfully privileged race, into whose ear they could, when suffering under any illegal or unusual degree of oppression, without danger, pour their complaints. Through the mediation of this patron, not only was the conscience of the master often induced to listen to the dictates of justice or mercy ; but the protection of the magistrate was sometimes invoked with safety to the complainants, against such wrongs as the law would redress.

By these causes, not only was their attachment to, and zeal for, religion promoted, but that reverence which the Romish tenets and ceremonies are strongly calculated to secure to the priesthood, was naturally encreased ; so that the clergy had a very powerful influence upon the minds of the

slaves ;

slaves; and the effect survived at St. Domingo the revolution which gave them their freedom; for the priests were notoriously in high favour with Toussaint, and were supposed greatly to influence his councils. The popularity of the clergy has since no doubt been much impaired; but it is probably not entirely lost; for though some of the body, seem to have become the dupes, or willing instruments, of the Consul's perfidious policy, the greater part of them it is fair to presume, have deplored the vile measures of the government; and if they durst not oppose, have at least not openly involved themselves in its crimes. But at all events, if the religious principle has survived among any large portion of the people, it will be a necessary effect of the Romish faith, to restore the influence of the priesthood.

To the independency of the new society, the clergy will probably feel no disinclination, provided it can be placed under the safeguard of a powerful guarantee; but if not, their prudence, and their European feelings, will conspire with their predilections as Frenchmen and Catholics, to make them desirous of a reconciliation with the Republic:—Their powerful influence therefore may in that case be expected to favour any agreement which France may propose; at least if it be not inconsistent with the freedom and happiness of their converts.

Nor

Nor are these the only adherents by whom the Indigenes are likely to be influenced in favour of a compromise with France, should we leave them unoccupied by a better exterior connection. They have European inmates and fellow soldiers, whose superior knowledge and talents must naturally have great weight in their public councils ; and to these, an equivocal or irresolute conduct on our part in regard to the independency of the new state, will create an evident necessity of making their peace with France. The Polish, Italian, and French deserters, and even such of the planters, who either from the first opposed the violent measures of the government, or forsook the sinking cause of Rochambeau, are now of course inimical to, and proscribed by, the consular government. The situation of these men must at present be one of considerable uneasiness and anxiety ; for though they were induced by prudence, or driven by oppression, or by just horror at the crimes of the Consul, to forsake the execrable standard of the French army, and join the insurgents, it must be an alarming consideration with them that they are at present cut off from every European community, and embarked in a cause which no civilized state has yet patronized or acknowledged ; at the peril, on the one hand, of the popular jealousy to which their complexion exposes

poses them among their new associates, and on the other, of the indignation of the Consul, and the perils perhaps of a new invasion. To such men, nothing could be more desirable than to see the freedom and independency of St. Domingo taken under the protection of Great Britain; but should they find that all our animosity to the Republic, will not induce us at this most favourable juncture, to coalesce with an African people in the Antilles, they will perceive that an accommodation with France, can alone deliver them from the dangers of their present situation. They will therefore be eager to make their peace with the existing or some future government of that country; and will be glad to purchase their pardon, by using all their influence to bring over the African chiefs to such a compromise as may be safely recommended.

From these united considerations I infer, that you ought not to rely on the present great and just exasperation of the people of St. Domingo, as full security against the attempts of France to regain their dependency as colonists ; much less against the wiser endeavour on her part, to obtain their friendship and alliance.

There is, however, at this critical juncture, a principle far more influential upon the new society than the motives and the interests to which
I have

I have adverted, and all other popular feelings united; and by this, if wisely enlisted on our side, you may raise insuperable bars to their future re-union with France, and perpetuate their animosity to that country You have only to appeal to that heart-stirring feeling, their solicitude for the safety of freedom, their dread of " the horrible yoke," and bid them to look to our maritime power, for the protection at once of their private liberty, and their independency as a nation. Guarantee those important objects— make the price of the stipulation a perpetual alliance against France—and their breach with her will be widened so extensively as to close no more. The Republic will thenceforth have nothing to concede, that will not be regarded as already securely obtained—no offers to make, that will not be considered as insidious,—no menaces to use, but such as will be despised.—Then indeed, you may rely upon the lasting effect of the Consul's cruelties and frauds, may pronounce a final divorce between this injured people and their merciless oppressors, and effectually say, " *pugnent ipsi nepotes.*"

A treaty or an intercourse merely commercial, would be so far from producing these important consequences, that our disposition to form such relations, and to stop short at that point, might

furnish

furnish arguments against us to the advocates of
the Republic   Such a half measure under present
circumstances, might speciously, nay, it might
truly, be represented, rather as a proof of our incurable hostility to the freedom of the African
race in the Antilles, than any symptom of a contrary disposition. That we advanced so far, might
be reasonably ascribed to commercial cupidity ;
that we offered no closer relations, could only
be accounted for by what may be too fairly im-
puted to us, a bigoted antipathy to the new order
of things in St. Domingo.

The violent and acrimonious nature of our present
contest with the Republic, would add great force to
such an inference. Our abstemiousness in such a
case, could admit but of one solution, a solution so
obvious, that neither the emissaries of France, not
the sincere friends of the Indigenes, would fail,
to point it out to them.—" England, it would be
" said, is again practising the policy she used
" towards Toussaint.—She will take your com-
" merce during the war, but leave you exposed
" again at its conclusion, to all the vengeance of
" the Republic. Nay, she will perhaps again fa-
" cilitate even at the expence of her own imme-
" diate security, new efforts of that power against
" your freedom, by allowing French fleets to pass
" the ocean, prior to a definitive treaty, in order that
" you may the more effectually be surprised by a
                                        " powerful

" powerful invasion. She withholds the recogni-
" tion of that independency which you now assert
" against France, and avoids an alliance with
" you, in order that she may play again this
" part, without incurring the reproach of open
" perfidy. Nothing, therefore, remains to you,
" but to secure, at the expence of this selfish and
" bigoted nation, such good terms as you may
" now make with the republic."

If we would estimate rightly the probability of
a reconciliation between St. Domingo and France,
and form adequate conceptions of the mischievous
tendencies of such an event, we must look beyond the period of the present war.

At this moment any conciliatory efforts which
the French government might be disposed to
employ, however favoured by the hesitating conduct of this country, and by the particular interests of individuals in the colony, would be made
under such great disadvantages, as might very
probably render them abortive. The injured colonists would naturally regard them as the result
of a necessity imposed upon their late oppressors
by the renewal of a maritime war, and as mere stra-
tagems of a temporising policy; and there would
be no immediate dread of a hostile alternative, to
second the other motives which might incline them
towards an amicable settlement; but when the sea

N   shall

shall again be open to the enterprises of the Republic, she will be able to offer to them the olive branch with a better grace, and with a far more powerful effect. The recollection of past horrors even will then plead on the side of peace, and if no dangerous confidence be demanded, may contribute powerfully to silence the lingering voice of hatred and revenge. Should the French government then be prudent enough not to demand the admission of any army, or the submission to any exercise of its authority in matters of interior legislation or police, its sovereignty might very probably be acknowledged; but the closest fœderal connection at least, would hardly be refused. Indeed I see not how a reconciliation on such a basis, could at that period possibly be declined: for some exterior connection, of a commercial nature, would be indispensably necessary to the welfare of the new people themselves; and no other power could then venture to accept the advantages of their commerce, since France, as against other nations, would assert to it an exclusive, and indisputable title.

" But will not the supposed reconciliation be " innoxious to this country, when our dispute " with the Republic shall end?" Such a thick haze of prejudice and ignorance always hangs over the horizon of our colonial interests, that I

should

should not wonder were this question to arise in the mind of a British politician. But unless our next peace with France is to be eternal, and unless she shall lay down together with the sword, all her disposition to impair the commercial and colonial interests of this country, the restitution of her authority or influence at St. Domingo would be not less formidable to us after, than before, the termination of the war. To demonstrate this proposition would be easy; but it would be to lengthen an argument already too long for your time, if not for your patience. Besides, it is a work which has been anticipated in my former letters *, and if any part of the reasoning contained in them met a pretty general assent, it was that, as I have ground for believing, which applied to this part of my subject. To the Crisis of the Sugar Colonies, therefore, I beg leave to refer, for the probable effects of negro liberty in St. Domingo, when associated with the power, and directed by the councils of France.

To suppose that the Republic will, at the close of her present war with this country, choose rather to embark in a new crusade against liberty in the West Indies, than acquiesce in its establishment, would be to deem the madness of the Consul quite incurable; or if such a choice be expected

* Crisis, p. 85 to 93.

from

from the successors of that despot, it must be from the belief that Frenchmen in general are infected with the same disease; for never was interest more palpable than that which the Republic now has in supporting at St. Domingo the system she has vainly attempted to subvert; nor did experience ever attest any truth more clearly, than the impracticability of the opposite course.

But let it be supposed that the preposterous project of restoring slavery in that great island, will indeed be revived. In that case, an early reconciliation between the black colonists and France is not, I admit, to be apprehended : but will there be no danger to this country, from the new and furious contest which must inevitably ensue? Will our own colonies stand safe within the wind of such contention?

Here again I must use the right of referring to arguments which were offered two years ago to the public *. In calculating the probable effects of the then depending French expedition against St. Domingo, and of the armaments which were preparing to follow it, I pointed out the perilous consequences to which our colonies would, in either event of the contest, be speedily exposed; and shewed that if the attempt of the Consul

* Crisis, Letter 3d.

should

should prove successful, the new situation of
affairs in the West Indies would be such as to
place continually at the mercy of an ambitious
and perfidious power, our most valuable transat-
lantic possessions.

The reality of those grounds of alarm was, I believe, very generally felt, and the defensive precautions employed upon the Jamaica station,
evinced that they were not wholly disregarded by
his majesty's ministers.

If the arguments here referred to were con-
vincing in the month of March, 1802, they cannot be less so at this period; for intermediate events
have not tended to detract from their force:
every incident, on the contrary, of the war of
St. Domingo, and every official letter from the
French commanders, might be invoked to verify
the grounds of apprehension in question, as they
were stated in the Crisis *.

Cast

---

* I abstain, in general, from extracts ; but as a striking confirmation of one of the opinions here referred to, viz. that
France, if successful in her war with the negroes, would alledge, and really find, a necessity of forming such a military
establishment in St. Domingo, as would enable her, at the
commencement of a new war, to overwhelm our colonies
by a sudden and irresistible invasion, I request attention to
the following parallel passages.

Crisis, p. 97.	Le Clerc's Letter of March 26, in the Moniteur of May 22 t, 1802.
" I pretend not to determine, to " what extent her permanent mili- " tary establishment must necessa- " rily	" I hope that the divisions of " Flushing and Havre, that which " you

Cast your eye then once again, sir, over the pages to which I have referred, and estimate coolly, with the aid of that light which has been since afforded by experience, the probable effects of a new war between France and her revolted colonists. Though the renewal of such a contest, and with the same extreme and irrational object, on the part of France, to exasperate the quarrel, is a supposition sufficiently wide of probability, let it be made; and add, if you please, that the obstinate resistance of the black colonists will at length be overcome, and the old system restored. This was the supreme object of the vows of our plan-

---

" rily be enhanced ; it is sufficient
" to say, that beyond the defence
" of the old fortifications, endan-
" gered perpetually by a new in-
" ternal enemy, she must establish
" and maintain a military organi-
" zation in the interior, ramified
" enough, and strong enough, to
" overawe the slaves, and to give
" security and confidence to the
" masters, without this the coun-
" ter-revolution, we are supposing
" would be fruitless of every thing
" but blood; and with a permanent
" force like this at her command,
" no hostile neighbour could be safe
" for a moment. Draughts that
" would hardly be missed from such
" an establishment, would be ade-
" quate to overpower the strongest
" garrison we ever maintained dur-
" ing peace, in the largest of our
" islands."

" you announced to me from Brest,
" and that from Toulon, will spee-
" dily arrive. They will be use-
" ful to us, by enabling us to oc-
" cupy cantonments upon all the
" points of this vast colony ; which
" is the only means of arriving at
" the re-establishment of order and
" tranquillity."

On this head general Le Clerc's word may be taken—yet he probably had, at the date of this letter, at least thirty thousand men under his command.

ters

ters and slave traders ; " the consummation de-
" voutly to be wished ;" and let them again cheat
themselves and others if they can, with the hope of
such an event. But surely the British statesman will
no longer be their dupe, to such a pitch of credulity,
as to see in this phantom any promise of national
welfare. The problem has now been practically
solved ; and it is no longer matter of argument,
but of experience, that France cannot reduce to
submission, much less keep in subjection, the negroes of that large island, but by means utterly
inconsistent with the security of the British West
Indies. To facilitate, therefore, or permit such
a conquest, would be to prepare for an ambitious
and unprincipled enemy, the same military preponderance in the Antilles, that he already possesses
in Europe ; and wilfully to subject ourselves to the
ruinous necessity of maintaining large fleets and
garrisons during peace as well as war, in that destructive climate.

Yes, Sir, whatever be the interest of the
planter in this question, that of the nation is at
length become obvious and undeniable. Unless
the other powers of Europe would give a guarantee in respect of St. Domingo, which they refused for Malta, it is not safe for this country that
France should possess that large island again, by
such means as must certainly be employed for
the

the purpose. We must not again suffer fifty or sixty thousand French troops to be transported, to the West Indies; for we cannot rely that the folly and bigotry of the present, or any future French government, will again deliver us from the jeopardy of such an experiment. Had not the present war arrived in time to stop the pretended Louisiana expedition, we might have found that even the proud and inexorable Consul, when on the point of a new quarrel with this country, could have sacrificed his thirst for African blood, to his hatred of England; and found better employment for his recruited army, than hunting down with blood hounds their human game among the Mornes of St. Domingo *.

Between

* There is abundant reason to conclude that the great armament which was preparing during several months in the ports of Holland, and which was anxiously represented in the French gazettes, as destined for Louisiana, was in truth intended for St. Domingo. That the Consul should needlessly send a large army, which by the best conjecture I can form would have consisted of about twenty thousand men, with a train of artillery, and large magazines of ordnance and military stores, merely for the purpose of receiving possession of a ceded colony, and this at a time when the commanders in St. Domingo were urgently demanding reinforcements, which from the disposition of the army he found it difficult to send, is too unnatural to be credited.—No resistance could be feared on the part of the Spaniards, and a single frigate with the governor and his staff would have sufficed

Between the opposite extremes of the victory,
and the defeat of France, in her late contest at St.
Domingo, or rather between the conquest and
total

ficed for the pretended purpose ; but if not, at least the ships
would have been dispatched separately, or in small squadrons,
as soon as they were ready for the voyage ; instead of being
detained as they were, at the expence of great inconvenience
and delay, in order to be collected in a large fleet, till sick-
ness at length broke out among the troops, and the sea stores
became unfit for service. If New Orleans was the true
port of destination, all the evils of trans-marine expeditions
in time of war, were wantonly and preposterously incurred in
time of peace.

Besides, we have since had ample accounts from Louisiana,
and it has not transpired that any preparations were made for
the reception of a French army there, or that the arrival of an
armament so long preparing, and so accidentally delayed in
Europe, had there been at all an object of public expectation ;
whereas it has clearly appeared from intercepted letters, that
the promise of a new and powerful army had at that period
been made to the French commanders in St. Domingo, and
was indispensably necessary for the further conduct of the
war in that quarter.—When to these and other considerations,
we add the known necessity under which the Consul laboured, of concealing from the soldiers, whom he devoted to West
Indian service, the fatal field in which they were to be employed, and that Louisiana was the most convenient mask for
this purpose, there will remain little or no room to doubt,
that the fleet from Holland would have stopped short of the
mouth of the Mississippi, and landed its army at Cape Francois.

But was there no ulterior object ?—Beyond doubt, if the
desperate contest with the negroes was to be persisted in,
the new army would have found full and final employment
O in

total loss of the island, there was a possible middle
event, the effects of which were also considered in
the Crisis *, and they were shewn to be still more
dangerous

in St. Domingo; and it is, I admit, probable enough from
the Consul's character, that he would have continued enor-
mously to drain the bravest blood of the Republic without remorse, in the pursuit of his nefarious object. But, on the
other hand, there are some strong grounds for suspecting,
that this profound dissembler had a design at this period to
abandon an attempt which he at length found would be ineffectual; and that instead of obtaining, at the expence of a
new army, the chance of recovering a desart in St. Domingo,
he would by means of his new expedition, and the garrisons
of that island united, have contrived to seize by surprise upon
Jamaica; perhaps also on some of our other sugar colonies.

To give all the reasons that might be offered in support of
this suspicion, would be to enlarge this note into a disserta-
tation. I shall only mention the following.

1st. It appeared by various accounts, that a large embar-
kation of cannon and artillery stores, was a part of the pre-
paratory measures for this new expedition; but as the negroes
had no artillery, and no longer kept the field in considerable
bodies, and as the plan for the new campaign was to hunt
them down, and exterminate them in the interior, this part
of the preparations, does not seem to point to such a war as
that of St. Domingo.

2dly. The delay in the Texel, if St. Domingo was the true
object, was of the most discouraging and fatal tendency to the
cause of the Republic in that island; but upon the hypothesis
we are considering, this effect was of little consequence; and
might have been well compensated by the encreased effect of
the blow to this country, since length of preparation encreased
the magnitude of the armament to be employed against us.

* Page 35 to 93.

3dly.

dangerous than either of the former, to the colonial interests of this country. I mean that of a compromise between the Republic and her sable opponents,

3dly. If the further prosecution of the war in St. Domingo was really designed, Buonaparte was persisting in that project to an extent, and by means, which were not satisfactory to the commanders employed : for though General Rochambeau had the promise of large reinforcements, he sent a short time prior to his knowledge of the present war, the most respectable and imposing deputation his army could furnish, with General Boyer, the second in command, at its head, to make personal remonstrances to the Consul. (This appears by the letter before referred to in page 20.) Now it is hard to believe that the Consul meant to work in opposition to all his own instruments, though it is by no means improbable on the other hand, that he would keep in his own breast to the last, or confide only to the commander of the intended expedition, the important secret of his designs against England.

4th. It was disclosed in the French newspapers, during the latter stage of the preparations in Holland, and immediately before the rupture with this country, that the celebrated Victor Hugues was appointed to the command of the expedition to Louisiana, and the government of that colony. A man less likely to promote the Consul's views at St. Domingo, or better fitted to conduct the supposed design against the British West Indies, could not possibly have been selected.

5th. The discontent and desertion of the troops which had formerly been trepanned into the horrible service of St. Domingo, and the avowed disgust of the military in general to that service, must have presented strong grounds of apprehension as to the conduct of the new army, when it should find itself brought by stratagem into the ports of that island ; but if at the same period, the conquest of the English colonies should
be

ponents, upon the basis of private freedom, after a bloody and indecisive contest—A new war might possibly be ended by such an adjustment, and

be disclosed to them as the alluring object of immediate service, discontent, it was probable, would immediately subside, and be converted into satisfaction and applause. The same critical period would also have presented a happy opportunity, for conciliating the black colonists upon the basis of freedom; and glossing over by a compromise, to which vengeance against England would have furnished a pretence, the dishonour of a defeat by such enemies.

I will only add, in the last place, that upon this hypothesis the conduct of the Consul towards this country will be found perfectly natural. He provoked a quarrel. by frequent insult, because he wished to be on such terms with us as would, in due time, furnish an apology for the meditated aggression. But he was at last very desirous to avoid an immediate rupture, because the Louisiana expedition had not yet departed from the Texel. His plan was broken by that bold, though tardy, decision of our ministry, which, by exceeding his calculations, placed him in a severe dilemma between his policy and his pride. He advanced, however, to the verge of extreme humiliation, in order to defer for a short time a war which all his previous conduct evinced a determination to provoke. St. Domingo alone could present no motive for such inconsistency. A brief interval of maritime peace, could there only have served to aggravate his loss, and his dishonour, while an immediate war with England was his best apology for defeat in that disastrous field, as well as the mean of saving a new army from useless destruction.

For these reasons I am strongly disposed to believe, that our complaint of preparations in the enemy's ports was not so groundless as is generally supposed; and that the measure anticipated

and a coalition between the two armies produce
that formidable union of European and African
arms, to the perilous effects of which I formerly
called your attention.

The fearful tendency of such a coalition is sufficiently obvious. It would give to the direction
of our inveterate enemy, means of future annoyance and conquest, to which the whole dis-
posable army of Great Britain, could it be spared
for West India service, might be vainly opposed. It would make the establishment of
French dominion through the whole chain of the
Antilles, a matter of such obvious facility, that
the most moderate of governments might find
it hard to resist the temptation.

Is it thought more likely, that the negroes, should
they again triumph over the new efforts of France,
would become, by new provocations, too much ex-
asperated against her to be afterwards the willing
instruments of her ambition, either as her political
dependents or allies? You would, even by this most
favourable result, be at best only replaced in the
situation, and restored to the happy opportunity
which you at present possess; you would still be
obliged to acquiesce in the establishment of an

anticipated in the Crisis, p. 90 to 92, was on the point of being
adopted by France, when averted by the recommencement of
war.

African

African power in the Antilles; and all the evils, real
or imaginary, which that innovation may threaten,
would at least remain undiminished.

But the case would, supposing it to arise in time
of peace, have this fearful aggravation—that the
remedy I now offer would be then unattainable,
except at the price of a new war with the republic; for you could not hope to be permitted by
that power to form any amicable connections
with her late subjects, either political or commercial; and to treat with them without such permission, would reasonably be regarded as highly af-
fronting and injurious.

It cannot be thought that, when obliged to
desist from the new war with her colonists, she
would make a gratuitous grant of their independency; since no regard to her own security
would demand such a sacrifice. She has, let
it be considered, no colony to the leeward of
St. Domingo; and her windward islands are
divided from it, not only by a long tract of sea,
which, from the constant course of the trade winds,
forms a very sufficient barrier; but by many intermediate colonies of England, Denmark, and Spain.
Having therefore no offensive enterprises to fear
from these sable enemies, and no commerce which
they will have power to annoy, the Republic will,
in the event last supposed, find no motive for a pacification

cification on the basis of independency, unless the
very advantages which I would now persuade
you to secure to ourselves, shall be conceded to
her by her late subjects, as the substitutes for
her title to govern. To renounce her sovereignty
on cheaper terms, would be not only to deliver
our colonies from a nuisance; but to transfer to
this country or other nations, the trade and the
power of St. Domingo.

The course of conduct which France would pursue
in such a case therefore, would unquestionably be
this. She would withdraw her armies from the
island; but surround it, to our extreme inconvenience, with a powerful naval blockade; and having in right of her pacific relations with other
states, the power to exclude their interference,
would soon or late make the islanders glad to accept of peace and independence, on the terms
of granting to their former sovereign the monopoly of their trade, and engaging with her in a
perpetual treaty of offensive and defensive alliance.

In short, Sir, you would in this least adverse
event, for such, in comparison with a triumph of
the French arms in St. Domingo I have elsewhere
shewn it to be, gain only a brief respite to our colonies. You would not be able, as now, finally to
prevent the irresistible sword of negro freedom
from falling into the hands of France.

Take then, Sir, your choice of future prospects.

Place

Place yourself by anticipation in the act of nego-
tiating for a new peace, and look forward to
whichever of these consequences of the treaty
you deem the least to be deprecated. Expect the
future policy of the Republic to be of what character you please, just or nefarious, cautious or rash,
rational or absurd;—suppose as you please, either
that she will, or that she will not attempt to
coerce and subjugate by new armies the people
of St. Domingo; and if such an attempt is
to be made, imagine it either to be, or not to
be, successful. In each of these cases, you
will be involved in some of those dangerous
consequences to which I have adverted, and the fearful extent of which was demonstrated in my
former address.

Of all the considerations then by which my advice may be supported, the most powerful is that
which an adversary perhaps might adduce on the
opposite side :—*to avoid difficulties in the next
pacification with France*, you should not lose a
moment in acknowledging the independence, and
securing the alliance of St. Domingo.

" What," I seem to hear some timid politician
exclaim, " will you obstruct our path to peace by
" new obstacles ! Have we not differences enough
" already to adjust with France, without revolting
" her pride, by demanding the abdication of her
" most important colony ?"

With

With such Englishmen, if any there be, as are
prepared to accept from our haughty enemy unequal and unsafe conditions of peace, I desire not
to reason—they may be disposed, for ought I
know, to renounce all our West Indian colonies,
rather than protract the present arduous contest:
but for my own part, I see no prudent medium,
between truckling to our insolent enemy at once,
and exacting from him such conditions, as are
compatible with our own future security, abroad,
as well as at home. I am sure too, that this commercial country is not yet prepared to give up her
trans-atlantic possessions, as the price of the amity
of the Great Nation; and therefore if peace were
worth the sacrifice of honour and security, it would
still, in my opinion, be unwise to leave France in
possession of a title to St. Domingo; because that
title would soon be the means of engaging us,
for the preservation of our sugar colonies, in
a new and more formidable war. If we must
have a West Indian cause of hostilities with the
Republic, I would rather it should be such a cause,
as would place the arms of the Indigenes, and the
interests of the African race, on our side, than one
that would range them both under the standard
of our enemies.

I presume not to say at what exercise of our
indubitable rights, the arrogant pride of France

P   may

may not be offended; but this I will affirm, that the measure in question, will give her no just or specious ground of complaint.

To support the revolting members of a hostile state, is an unimpeachable exercise of the rights of war. By our Elizabeth, and by the Great Henry of France; such policy was practised without scruple; and the haughty Philip was obliged to sheath his sword without avenging the affront. But of the numerous precedents that might be adduced, the conduct of France herself. in the American war, is at once the most appropriate and recent; and surely the pride of a French government may fairly brook, what Great Britain herself was obliged to digest, little more than twenty years ago.

It is, however, wronging the argument to compare these two cases; for France had no pretence of any necessity, arising out of the care of her own security, when she acknowledged, and engaged to defend, the independency of the United States; whereas the preservation of our most valuable colonies, demands from us an alliance with St. Domingo. I might add, that the one measure was a violation of the duties of peace : while the other, if now adopted, will be the act of an open enemy, possessing all the rights of legitimate war.

But independently of all precedent, and beyond the range of all ordinary principle, the proposed

posed treaty might be justified, if necessary, upon the very singular nature of the case.

France, by her own act, whether intentionally or through the unforeseen effect of her domestic revolutions, is immaterial, has created a new political power in the Antilles; a power dangerous perhaps in itself, but which in her hands would inevitably be destructive, to the security of its colonial neighbours. She has therefore imposed upon us a necessity of treating this new power as independent; and of engaging it, if we can, in such connections, as may exclude her influence or authority over it in future.

Nor is it material to this ground of defence, that the Republic should be considered as still wishing to maintain that work of colonial revolution, which she once openly abetted. The case to be sure would in that case be stronger against her : for such policy might, upon views lately professed by herself, be justly regarded, as a direct attack upon the security of other powers, in their West Indian possessions; as an injurious violation, to use the words of Villaret, " of those " principles, which alone can preserve, and upon " which reposes, the common interest of all the " European powers in their establishments in the " Antilles*."

* Villaret's letter to the British admiral at Jamaica, on the arrival of the first expedition at Cape Francois, February 14, 1802.

The

The author trusts he cannot be suspected of concurring in the principle of this quotation. He is far from thinking, that the powers of Europe have a common interest, any more than a common right, in maintaining and perpetuating a system of the most odious and impolitic oppression, that ever afflicted or disgraced humanity. But he reasons to many who may differ from him, perhaps, on this subject; and as between the nations who still uphold that loathsome despotism, the reasoning is undeniably fair.

But it is enough, that what France did, or permitted in St. Domingo, she is found unable to repair. Whatever self conservatory rights the innovation gave to us, they cannot be taken away by an ineffectual attempt to reverse it, and to restore the former state of things; for that fruitless effort has not removed or diminished the danger, against which we are driven to provide. A man who should wilfully or carelessly set fire to his own house, would thereby give his neighbours a right to pull it down, if such a subversion of his property, were necessary to the preservation of their own. Could he plead inevitable accident in his excuse; the right, though it might be more tenderly exercised, would not be taken away. But to say, that he had already done all in his power to extinguish the flames without success, would

clearly

clearly be to strengthen, rather than impair, the right of his neighbours to apply the only effectual remedy. What should we say, were he in such a case to claim a right to lock up his doors, to forbid our ascending the roof, and to insist, in all points, on the exercise of his former dominion, as owner of the tenement ?

It may be said, that this illustration proves rather a right in other nations to effect, if they can, a counter revolution in St. Domingo, than to treat it as independent; on the same principle upon which the late confederated powers of Europe, might have justifiably restored, if they could, the monarchy of France. But I answer, that supposing such a work really capable of being accomplished, and at an expence which other nations could afford, and which they could be reasonably called upon to sustain, there are, in this case, third parties, in respect of whom very serious moral difficulties must first be removed. Such a remedy, however, is demonstrably impracticable. Even were it fit that the blood, the treasure, and the conscience of Great Britain, should be sacrificed to the effecting, for the benefit of France, the re-establishment of the old system in St. Domingo, she has not power to accomplish such a work. She must therefore resort to the only attainable security against that,

which

which is in truth the worst part of the danger, the power of annoyance which the new state of things is likely to impart hereafter to an envious rival, and an insidious enemy. The conflagration in this case is to be dreaded, chiefly through that connection with France, which is likely to carry the flames. To pull down the roof and walls of that connection therefore, not to subvert the fabric of African freedom or independency, is the precaution towards which our efforts must be directed, and which we have an incontestable right to adopt.

Were we now at peace with the Republic, these reasons might justify, perhaps, our entering into an alliance with her late subjects of St. Domingo. They might at least justly warrant our demanding, as an alternative to that measure, good security against the dangers to which, either by a renewal of her quarrel with the new people, or by a compromise of the subject of that quarrel, we must unavoidably be exposed. But happily, I write at a time when the measure in question can, in point of moral rectitude, demand no such arguments in its defence. To the right of self-preservation we need not now resort; nor to any moral consequences deducible from the past conduct of France; since the comprehensive rights of war, clearly entitle us to treat with a revolted
colony

colony of our enemy, and to sever it finally, if we can, from his dominions.

That a French government would hereafter reject terms of peace, which might in other respects be mutually acceptable, on the score of our having become allies of St. Domingo, and guaranteed its independence, is highly improbable. But if a renunciation of her claim to that potent and menacing island, be requisite for our future security, it must of course be demanded from her in the next negotiation for peace, although we should not be previously bound by treaty, to prescribe to her such a condition : and the only question in this case is, whether the condition would be more offensive, and obstruct longer the important work of pacification, because during a time of hostility, we had contracted engagements which bound us to insist upon it, and from which we could not, without dishonour, recede.

That the contrary would rather be the effect of such engagements, may safely be affirmed. National pride would be less mortified, and the credit of a minister far less impaired, in such a case, by acquiescing in relations already formed, and engagements already contracted and irrevocable, than by giving way to new pretensions, and allowing an enemy to obtain as the price of peace, more than he had ventured to lay claim to during all the acrimony of war.

France

France herself understands the value of this distinction, and therefore openly bound herself during the late war in compacts with the people she conquered, not only to maintain them in their revolt from their ancient sovereigns, but to retain them as dependants on, or integral parts of, the Great Nation. Far different indeed, was this audacious proceeding, from the just and necessary measure, which I would persuade you to adopt; yet these covenants of usurpation were alledged by the French government itself, in the subsequent negotiations for peace, and perhaps not without advantage. The self-imposed necessity of demanding extreme concessions, served probably, in some slight degree, to soften to the feelings of the despoiled and injured powers, the arrogant pretensions of the Republic; or at least, by precluding the hope of peace on cheaper terms, made them submit a little sooner than they would otherwise have done, to the urgent calls of necessity.

A case more nearly parallel, is to be found in the peace which terminated the American war; and I appeal to the feelings of Englishmen, whether that contest would have ended so soon, had France previously avoided an alliance with our colonies during the war, and afterwards demanded their independency, or security against their re-union with this country, in the negotiations at Versailles.

Unless

Unless then, Sir, you are prepared to say, that the Republic, at the conclusion of the present war, ought to be left wholly unrestrained to act as her policy or ambition may suggest in relation to St. Domingo, you ought, even for the sake of future peace, to embrace the present opportunity. If there be no danger or inconvenience in again suffering large French armies to pass, during peace, into the centre of the Antilles, and if there be nothing to be apprehended from that far more probable event, the reconciliation of St. Domingo with France, you may safely proceed in your present equivocal conduct: but if the dangers pointed out to your notice in the Crisis of the Sugar Colonies, had any reality and importance, you should hasten to profit by the present opportunity, of preventing their future recurrence. By delay, you will not only risk all the inconveniences and evils which I have shewn to be the probable fruits of the present state of things in the West Indies during the war; but will enhance the difficulties that may oppose its safe and speedy termination.

To pursue to the same important period, the comparison between a commercial treaty, and a close political alliance, it should be observed, that the former would, in no degree, deliver us from the dilemma in a negotiation for peace, which

Q   the

the latter is calculated to avoid; and that the peculiar advantages of the one, cannot be expected to extend beyond the present war, without the aid of the other. Unless our next peace shall find, or place the inhabitants of St. Domingo, in a state of acknowledged independency, France certainly will not allow this country to trade to their ports: much less to do so with an exclusive preference, or in right of a treaty which would be derogatory from her sovereign authority. She will not, as I before remarked, spontaneously renounce her sovereignty, merely to legitimate our trade, and sanction our commercial privileges.

The four different projects which were originally proposed for consideration, have now been distinctly reviewed.

To prohibit all commercial intercourse between His Majesty's subjects, and the new masters of St. Domingo, has been shewn to be neither politic nor safe; and that such an intercourse, if carried on at all, ought to be sanctioned and regulated by treaty, has, I hope, been sufficiently proved. But whether our commercial intercourse with that people should be confined to commercial objects, or should extend to a political league of the nature I would persuade you to form,

seemed

seemed the question most open to dispute. Those rival projects therefore have been more amply considered, and their respective pretensions compared.

The practical result, if I have reasoned satisfactorily, is this—That a treaty with the people of St. Domingo, involving a recognition of their independence, and a perpetual alliance against France, ought to be negotiated without a moment's delay. No measure less decisive, will secure to you the future commerce of that valuable island—No other expedient, will guard our sugar colonies so effectually from the evils with which they are menaced.—No connection less intimate, will deliver you during the present and future wars, from the maritime inconveniences to be dreaded from the independence of St. Domingo, and its new relations towards other powers; much less secure to you the important belligerent advantages, which its amity is likely to produce.

But the grand consideration of all, is the highly probable, and most pernicious alternative to this alliance, a reconciliation between the new people and France. That they may not speedily become your formidable enemies, you must make them your obliged allies. You must guarantee their independence against the Republic, that they may not, to the ruin of your colonies, fall

in

in their enfranchised state, and with their new-born energies, under her dominion, or her influence. Of such a reconciliation there is danger perhaps even at the present moment; but upon the conclusion of the war, at latest, such an event will almost infallibly ensue, unless precluded by the wise measure which I advise you now to adopt. Supposing the Republic even to be rash enough to recur to her counter revolutionary efforts, the folly would only retard, not ultimately prevent, a coalition fatal to our colonies, would subject them to new intermediate perils, and leave them exposed in the sequel, to dangers not less imminent than those with which they are at present menaced, without leaving a British minister at liberty to employ those means of prevention, which may now be unobjectionably used.

The evils therefore which exist, and those which are likely to arise, the dangers of the war, and those to which peace will give birth, admit but of one remedy; are to be prevented or lessened by one only expedient. If you would wield the sword without new disadvantages, if you would sheath it without peril to our colonies, and if you would diminish the difficulties which oppose the restitution of peace, you must embrace without delay, the present opportunity; you must adopt
the

the measure I propose. A wall of perpetual separation between France and St. Domingo must necessarily be built; and therefore the liberty and independency of the new people must be acknowledged, and must be placed under British protection. By that wise use of the present opportunity, and by that mean alone, the great revolution which has taken place in the West Indies, an event pregnant perhaps with grander, and more lasting effects, than any of the late revolutions of Europe, may be rendered wholly innoxious, nay, largely beneficial to this country; and pernicious only to that unprincipled power, which first rashly made, and then wickedly tried to reverse it.

I hasten to lay down the pen, lest before these arguments shall meet your eye, the opportunity they relate to should be lost; but it seems necessary to notice briefly, before I conclude, some general prepossessions, by which my advice may perhaps be fatally opposed.

A contempt, not less irrational, than cruel for the much injured African race, has, I fear, through the prejudiced and self-interested representations of their oppressors, been strongly impressed upon the public mind in this country.

From this sentiment indeed, the sable defenders

ers of St. Domingo must now have delivered themselves in every generous breast—But the malice of their enemies is unwearied ; and though it is now hopeless to represent them as a despicable groveling race, fit only for the harness of a brutal bondage, and likely again to submit with tameness to the whip of the driver ; it is attempted, not, I fear, without success, to pourtray them as ferocious and merciless savages, unfit to maintain the pacific relations of independency with other states, or even to adhere to each other, in any firm political union ; as incorrigible barbarians, who will soon split into petty hordes, and relapse into African manners.

Were there any sound foundation for these notions, the force of some of the motives which I have offered for an alliance with the New State, would certainly be weakened; yet more than enough would remain to support the practical conclusion. As an experiment at least, and as a temporary expedient, it would still be right to make friends of those, who whether barbarous or civilized, may be troublesome and dangerous enemies : nor would their ferocity, I presume, render them instruments less terrible of the future machinations of France, should she be able to employ them against our colonies.

But this portrait of the brave Indigenes is traced

ed by the pencil of prejudice; and this prediction of their future fate, is rather the voice of a venal oracle, bribed by their oppressors; than the legitimate foresight of reason, derived by fair calculation from historical truth.

If we consider in the first place, their treatment of their vanquished enemies, at and immediately after the surrender of the towns, we shall discover no traits of inhumanity. Reasonably enough did the French garrisons, and their white adherents, expect a dreadful retaliation; for never had cruelty or perfidy, in the conduct of a war, been carried to fouler extremes, than by them or their execrable leaders : nor is there upon earth, perhaps, to be found a people by whom, when outraged by such unparalleled wrongs, the expectation might not have been fully and immediately realized? Yet not a single drop of blood was vindictively shed upon the occupation of those towns by the Negroes.

British humanity indeed in one or two cases interposed, and complaisance to our commanders may be thought solely to have influenced the conduct of the Negro chiefs; but it remains to be proved, that without such interposition, the garrisons or inhabitants would have been put to death, or unmercifully treated; and the contrary is fairly presumable from the event at those places, where the surrender was made, not to British
officers,

officers, or under British mediation, but immediately to the African besiegers.

Cape Francois was obliged to capitulate, in consequence of a most gallant and successful assault made by Dessalines, upon the hill forts which command that town. The capitulation was afterwards broken by Rochambeau, who omitted to evacuate the town within the stipulated time; and it seems to be the import of our own official accounts, that the place was ultimately taken by storm; for Dessalines marched hostilely into the town, to enforce the departure of the garrison: consequently the capitulation was totally void, and whatever mercy the inhabitants received, they owed to his clemency alone. It is not pretended that in this case the extreme right of a victor, was waived in complaisance to the British; and it on the contrary appears, that an exemption of the ships from destruction by the batteries on shore, was all we obtained, or treated for. Rochambeau, who having broken his faith, was not intitled to withdraw the garrison or the ships, saved himself and them, by a tardy surrender to the British blockading force*, but left the inhabitants to the mercy of the victors.

Yet

---

* See the London Gazette of February 7th, 1804. Dessalines seems at this period to have been dissatisfied with the conduct of our commanders, and to have reluctantly permitted

Yet they were all spared, and treated, for a long
time at least, with the utmost humanity *.

At

ted the execution of the compact between them and Rochambeau. But it is impossible, considering our conduct at other
places, to be surprized at, or blame this disposition in the
Negro Chief, or his refusal to assist our ships in entering the
port by sending them pilots. *He probably had still stronger
reasons for distrust than are yet before the public :* but it was
enough, that our system evidently was not only to dismantle
their forts, and destroy their works, for which the fear of their
re-occupation by France might furnish a slight pretence; but
to carry away their ammunition and military stores ; for which
no pretence compatible with sincere amity could be found.
Dessalines therefore was probably actuated as much by humanity, as by complaisance for our commanders, when he suffered the fleet to escape. He had, it is admitted, the power
of destroying them, as he was preparing to do, by red hot shot
from the batteries; and he had, as I conceive, an unquestionable
right so to act; in order to compel their surrender to himself, notwithstanding their having capitulated to the British squadron.
It is impossible to maintain that we had a right without
his leave so to rescue from his hands, an enemy who had
broken a prior capitulation with him, who then lay at his
mercy, and who was not in a condition even to execute the
compact, by putting the ships into our possession, but by his
permission. If Dessalines did not act upon principles of moderation and mercy; his complaisance for this country was
extreme; and intitles him strongly to our favour.

* Various reports of a massacre at this town and other
places at a subsequent period, have been received from Jamaica
and North America.—See the London newspapers of the 3d
of May. I hope they will prove like a multitude of similar
reports from the same quarters, to be either wholly groundless, or great exaggerations of the truth ; but considering the
unparalleled circumstances by which popular rage and panic

R   are

At Fort Dauphin, General Dumont and his staff, having been surprised in a sortie, had fallen into the hands of the besiegers, sometime prior to the capitulation to his Majesty's ships; but upon notice of that event, they were, at the request of a British officer, given up*. According indeed to our official account, this request was made in order to save them from the vengeance of the Negroes: but if such vengeance was impending over them, how happened it not to have been executed? These allies of the blood hounds, and conductors of an exterminatory war, were surely very fortunate, in being preserved alive, and unhurt, till British humanity could come to their aid, and provide for their ultimate safety. The vengeance of ferocious savages is not usually so very tardy.

At Aux Cayes, St. Marc's, Jeremie, and other captured Towns, a similar clemency was displayed; the Negro Chiefs openly challenged praise upon this ground, and by their enemies the claim was allowed †.

are likely to be excited, especially while the French still menace and annoy them from Cuba, such events are certainly not improbable.

* London Gazette of December 10, 1803.

† See a letter of Dessalines, and a proclamation of the Town Council of the Cape, in London newspapers of February 6.

To

[123]

To such instances of moderation and mercy at
the close of a most enfuriated contest, might be
added others not less striking, during the utmost
fury of the struggle. When a history of that
horrible war shall be published by less partial
editors than the writers of Buonaparte's gazettes, although with no sources of information
less inimical than those mendacious papers themselves, fairly compared with each other, the defence of this persecuted people may be made to
greater advantage, and it will appear that they
in general conducted themselves, through the
whole of that terrible contest, with a degree of
forbearance and humanity such as was never sur-
passed by any people upon earth.

All the white inhabitants of Cape Francois, for
instance, were confessedly in the power of Christophe, at the time of Leclerc's arrival; and when
the negro general, in obedience to his orders, and
conformably to the clearest principles of defensive
warfare, set fire to that town on his retreat into
the interior, to prevent its affording cover to the
invaders, it was at first alleged by the French, and
loudly echoed from Jamaica, and North America,
that he had put all the inhabitants to the sword.
Yet the contrary was soon acknowledged by his
enemies themselves — It was admitted in the
French

French gazettes that not one of these inhabitants had perished *.

We learn from the same authority, that a great portion of the French inhabitants, who were carried off from that and other towns and districts on the coast, and an aid-de-camp of General Boudet, remained in the custody of Toussaint among the mornes, during the whole of a dreadful campaign, in which his enemies, by their own avowal gave no quarter to his adherents: yet it is attested by the Moniteur itself, that they were all brought back in safety, when that hero at length sheathed his victorious sword on the faith of a treacherous compact †.

Surely such prominent and unquestionable facts as these should suffice, if not fully to vindicate the humanity of the African race, at least to discredit the channels of intelligence, through which the credulity of the English public has often been abused, and its feelings tortured, by shocking and false accounts of massacres in St. Domingo.

In some instances no doubt, the keen feelings of indignation, never surely in any age or country

* French accounts in London Newspapers of March 22, 1802; " *No person was killed at the Cape; every one came back into the Town.*"

† See London papers of June 17, 1802, and the Moniteur of June 14. " *All the planters who had been carried off are returned.*"

excited

excited by such cruel and flagitious injuries, have led the multitude to imitate the example of their European invaders; and to retaliate ten thousand massacres and murders, of which their brethren and dearest connections had been victims, upon Frenchmen that fell into their hands. But instead of exhibiting, in those trying scenes, a more than usual portion of human depravity, their forbearance on the whole, has been such as may justly excite surprise, and is not inconsistent with the praise bestowed upon their hapless race by travellers in their native Africa, that of being " the mildest of uncivilized men *."

Were

* To those who have been accustomed to read with implicit faith, the insertions in the French gazettes, or extracts from Jamaica or American newspapers, these propositions may appear very bold; but whoever will have the patience to look back upon those accounts, and compare them with each other, will find scarcely any accusation against the humanity of these brave men, that has not been refuted by subsequent information, even from the same hostile quarters; while he will find striking instances of their clemency and forbearance, stated on the authority of the French commanders themselves. Of the news from St. Domingo, received through the United States of America, it may truly be said, that it was in general less worthy of credit if possible than even the French gazettes; and to shew the falsehood of most of the shocking accounts copied from American prints, General Leclerc's own dispatches might suffice. It should be remembered, that there is in the United States a large party as much interested in vilifying the African character, as the people of Jamaica; perhaps still more so; on account of the great preponderance in that country

try

Were the defence of the humanity of this
people more difficult; still why the new masters
of St. Domingo must of necessity break that
bond

try of the party inimical to negro slavery, and the consequent
apprehension of slave owners, that the state will be wholly
abolished. The author is credibly informed that another motive for misrepresentation, often induces American masters and
merchants to spread false or highly exaggerated accounts of
horrors supposed to have been witnessed by them in St. Domingo, upon their return from that island. It is often an important commercial object to deter other merchants from sending cargoes to the same port to which they themselves have
been recently trading, or to which they mean to return.

After all, however, he desires not to be understood as abso-
lutely denying the truth of the rumours now current, relative
to recent massacres. If a proclamation of January 1st, ascribed
to Dessalines be authentic, such events must necessarily have
followed, though their horrors have probably been much enhanced by report, both in America and Jamaica. In this case
Dessalines is indeed a most unworthy successor of the humane
Toussaint ; but let the inflammatory language of that Proclamation be fairly considered (I will print it for the purpose in an
Appendix.) Next let the extreme excitement, of late injuries
and of present alarms be fairly estimated, and we shall find
more reason to think favourably of the people, to dispose
whom to vengeance such exhortation was necessary, and upon
whom its effects have been so tardy and incomplete, than to
ascribe to them an extraordinary ferocity. In two months it
seems not to have produced any outrages, except in the south
of the Island.

But it seems to be decisive of the general character of the
Negroes, that the *inhabitants of Cape Francois, to whom they
were best known, chose to remain in their power :* that it was
matter of election, or not of strict necessity, is certain.

See the capitulation, and other papers, in the London newspapers of February 6th.

bond of union which has hitherto bound them to each other, renounce those arts of civil life with which they are acquainted, and degenerate into absolute barbarism, is not easy to discover.

If we look to the peculiar disposition of negroes, or to the little we know of their history, there is nothing in either, from which the hopes of the enemies of their race can derive any support.

As to the miserable man-stealing districts on the coast of Guinea, I inquire not whether those contemptible factories, or rather those shambles, of our slave-traders, which are there mocked with the appellation of kingdoms, are increasing in number, by the splitting of their petty domains; but I believe no such fact is alledged. Certainly, it is the natural tendency of the foul crimes we instigate, to produce political disunion, as well as every other species of evil; but to judge of African character in general, from the inhabitants of that wretched border, would be as unreasonable in us, as it would be in them, to estimate christian morals, and British manners, from what they see of the Liverpool agents and captains. If the calumniators of Africa would point us to its miserable slave coast, for the proof of any of their pretences, let them first deliver it from the excitement of their own execrable commerce. Till then, a procuress might as fairly ask us to read

the

the character of our virtuous countrywomen, in the manners of her own brothel.

In the interior of that great continent, nations are known to exist, which unite in one·political body, and under a single head, millions of people, spread over a very extensive territory; and we are not told of any separation, or dismemberment, by which their magnitude has been lessened. I remember no relation from which it can be inferred that these nations have undergone any such changes, or that their unity is likely to be broken; and much less, that they have retrograded from any advances in civilization or arts which they may formerly have made: on the contrary, it appears, that in proportion as you recede from the western coast, and emerge from the foul haunts of European man-merchants, symptoms of advancing improvement in civilization, become very conspicuous. But were the case otherwise; still I demand, what are the facts in the history of mankind which warrant the expectation in question, as it applies to Africans already versed in the arts of agriculture and commerce, and formed into a single community?. Has it been the ordinary conduct. of unpolished societies, to burst the political bonds by which they have been once₍united, and to renounce the arts they have learned? The. institutions of Peter, have not been lost; and it might, for aught I know, be as safe to

guarantee

guarantee the integrity of Russia or Abyssinia, as of Germany or France.

If we look to the immediate subjects of this controversy, that portion of the African race, which has emerged in some degree from the artificial barbarism of the West Indies, we shall find still less reason for the opinion that their political concord will be broken, or that they will go backward in civilization.

That no symptoms of such disunion and retrogression have yet appeared, will, I presume, be admitted; for though several parties originally sprang up, as was natural, from the chaos of their great revolution, a centripetal attraction was from the first very active among them; and they were drawn by successive conjunctions, into circles more and more comprehensive till at length the whole population was united in one political system, under a single head; and this unity was afterwards maintained with the most perfect steadiness; in peace as well as in war, down to the moment of Leclerc's invasion.

Ambitious chieftains, once attempted to disturb it; but the effort was wholly fruitless. Their conspiracy was easily suppressed, by the mild but energetic policy of Toussaint; and even the disorganisers of Europe found it, upon their arrival, a difficult task, to divide by force and stratagem,

tagem, the well-knit fibres of this infant but vigorous frame.

Had divisions since prevailed, they would furnish but a feeble argument to support the opinion I am combating; for after insidious arts had seduced some of the negro chiefs to abandon for a while their illustrious leader, and after that great man himself had fallen a victim to the perfidy of Leclerc, the confidence of the distracted multitude could hardly find a pillar to rest upon; and the military dispositions of the enemy made union extremely difficult. It would not have been strange, therefore, had different chiefs erected several independent standards in different divisions of the island; and refused afterwards to acknowledge a superior, or to unite their authority when the common danger had subsided.

It was said, upon what evidence I know not, that a disunion of this nature had actually taken place; and that a large body of the negroes had agreed on an armistice with Rochambeau at the Cape. But if any such discord really arose, it appears to have had but a small extent, and a very brief duration; for no sooner did the surrender of the French troops open the way to accurate information, than we learned that the three principal chiefs, Dessalines, Christophe, and Clervaux, had united the whole island again under a single government,

vernment; over which, down to the period of the
latest advices, they continued jointly to preside.
In this triumvirate, Dessalines appears to take the
lead ; and it is worthy of remark, that he and
Christophe, were the most distinguished and
faithful officers of Toussaint.

That great man, it should be remembered, from
whom the Consul did not disdain to borrow the
plan of his present authority *, was elected governor for life, with a power to nominate his
successor ; but as the sudden act of perfidy by
which he lost his liberty and his life, precluded the
exercise of this power, a grateful people had no
better way to evince their reverence for his memory, and the stability of their social attachments,
than by ranging themselves under the standard
of those leaders, who held the chief authority under
him during his government, and had enjoyed the
largest share of his favour and confidence †. His

* While I write, rumour imports that this expression is in-
correct. It is said he is Emperor of the French. I must
hasten to publish, lest before my work appears he should
be deified ; and my strictures on his West-Indian policy
should outrage his humble worshippers, the free citizens of
the Great Nation.

† Again the course of events outstrips the progress of this
argument, but confirmsmy opinion.—It is reported, since the
above paragraph was ready for the Press, and apparently upon
good authority, that Dessalines is appointed sole Governor for
life.

oppressors

oppressors had taken care that there should be no hereditary representative, whom popular affection might have deemed a preferable object of choice.

I ask, then, what circumstance in the history of this new people warrants the conclusion that the union will not be lasting? Let a case be pointed óut, of a society now upon earth, or which ever existed, in which the principle of political cohe-sion has been more vigorous or perfect.

Other nations, let it be considered, have rarely, if ever, been formed under circumstances so unfa-vourable to the social union. They have either migrated under a single leader from other states, and a fœtus of civil or military organization has been formed, before the political birth : or they have been formed by gradual accretion, round a mucleus which originally possessed the organs of of municipal life ; or they have grown into a nation by the multiplication of a single family, of which the patriarchial government has de-scended upon the elder branch : but in St. Do-mingo, a new social edifice was to be raised at once, out of a mass of broken and heterogeneous ruins. In a moment, the petty thrones of some thousands of plantations were subverted, and half a million of enfranchised bondsmen, of as many different tribes and nations, and tongues, as the man-selling regions of Africa contain, were

were suddenly called upon to put on social character, to the first rudiments of which most of
them had, to that moment, been total strangers.

It would be but a faint image of this transition
to suppose the flocks and herds of Circe restored
in an instant to their pristine forms, and that
prior to their metamorphoses, they had arrived
from every different region of the eartn ; unless we
should add, that their numerous progeny, born
in a brutal form, and instructed only in the duties and manners of the stall, started into man-
hood along with them.

That men, under such circumstances, should
so soon and so abidingly unite themselves under
a single government, as the people of St. Domingo
did under that of Toussaint, is a prodigy which
strongly illustrates the force of those feelings
which attract and bind them to each other : but
to believe, after such an example, that negroes
are such savages as to be incapable of maintaining
their political union in the same identical island,
is to exhibit a prodigy of another kind, a preter-
natural extreme of credulity and prejudice.

I grant that the motives for union were in this
case exceedingly strong ; nay, I am ready to admit, that nothing but the unspeakable value, in a
physical as well as moral view, of negro freedom,
when compared with negro slavery, could possibly
have so soon produced, out of the vortex of anarchy,

chy, a union so perfect and tenacious. But will not the same peculiar motives still operate in favour of concord? I fear they will: for I have little expectation that Africans will soon find themselves safe in that part of the globe from the rapacious fangs of European avarice and despotism, except by that power of self-defence, which the Almighty has provided in his mercy for a united people every where, and especially for Africans between the tropics, against a European enemy. With the Indigenes, therefore, the dread of a horrible bondage will long be the cement of their political confederation.

Of a retrogression of this people from the point of civilization to which they have attained towards barbarism, there seems still less danger than of their political disunion. Under Toussaint, they advanced, as has been already noticed, both in agriculture and commerce; though never to be sure in the history of any society upon earth, was there a situation of affairs more adverse to that progress. Why then should we suppose that, when they are delivered from the miseries of civil and foreign war, and no longer agitated by the fear of a renovated slavery, they will neglect those grand sources of improvement?

Are they indolent? Indolence itself will plead for the culture of commercial articles. Their rich soil can supply their necessities, by means of its
exportable

exportable produce, at a less expence of labour, than it would cost them to provide in any other way, food, clothing, and other indispensable necessaries, even in the simplest style. Are they intemperate? The charge is in general false, insulting and preposterous; but I grant, that of those inebriating luxuries, in which their masters revelled, some of them occasionally obtained a taste, and have, doubtless, retained the relish. This vice, however, in the degree wherein it exists, will be a stimulus operating in favour of commerce; by which alone the means of indulging intemperance, and possessing the objects of luxury, can be obtained. Are they vain? I admit the imputation. They have no scanty share of that universal weakness. They love dress, in particular, in proportion to the difficulty with which the homely and tawdry attire which they used to be proud of, was acquired. Here the foreign merchant will have another hold upon them; a further allurement, exciting them to the preservation and extension of commerce, and of agriculture, as its necessary source.

To these impulses will be added, that which in a limited field, is perhaps the surest cause of agricultural improvement; a population rapidly encreasing; and likely, at no far distant period to exceed the number which the immediate produce of the soil could sufficiently sustain.

This

This cause, unless opposed by new territorial acquisitions, is likely to be peculiarly active and powerful at St. Domingo ; because from the great value of the exportable produce of a West India Island, when compared with that of the grain and other provisions imported in return for it, the effects of tillage in multiplying the means of support for a growing population, will there be peculiarly great and encouraging. It may be added, that as long as the complexion of the Indigenes shall constitute a legal presumption of slavery, and a brand of dishonour, in every West India island but their own, and almost in every civilized portion of the western world within the climate they love, they will have little inducement to lessen by migration these good effects of domestic encrease *.

The history of mankind in general, lends no countenance to the opinion I here combat.

* A free negro who travels in the West Indies, incurs a great risque of losing his liberty ; for by the laws of that country, the legal presumption is, that every black man or mulatto, is a slave, until the contrary appears ; and if his master be unknown, he is liable to be seized and sold for the use of the public. To avoid this, he must carry with him written testimonials of his enfranchisement ; but these may be lost or contested ; and the righteous law which lays the *onus probandi* upon him, has provided no means whereby he can make the proof required, or bring the question before any tribunal for discussion, unless benevolence should prompt some person incontestably free, to become his patron or guardian, and apply to the law on his behalf.

Often

Often have the arts of agriculture and commerce been chased away by barbarous invaders; and sometimes, as in Spain, they have declined through the depressing effects of bad civil institutions; but I can recollect no precedent in history, in which a people circumstanced like those of St. Domingo, have wholly abandoned those beneficial arts, and gone back into barbarous manners.

Indeed, history affords no case in which there has been half so much security against that unnatural retrogression. Not tempted by unlimited wastes, to engage in a wandering life; possessing but a moderate domain, where neither the hunter, nor the shepherd state, of uncivilized man, would find any local aptitudes; not cut off by deserts or forests from an intercourse with more polished societies; but placed in the very focus of the richest commerce upon earth, and circumscribed by a tranquil sea upon which the canvass of the merchant is perpetually visible from all points of their accessible coast; already expert in the arts of agriculture, and in the manufacture of its most valuable produce; already accustomed to the operations of commerce, and continually solicited to extend them ; if under circumstances like these, the Indigenes should expel those handmaids of civilization and social happiness, and degenerate into a savage state, the event would be strange indeed. Their stupidity might in that case half absolve the guilt of their op-

T   pressors,

pressors, and leave the slave trader little more to answer for at the bar of eternal justice, than the tormenting a mere animal existence, and the destruction of irrational life.

I will not enlarge these gratuitous arguments against an opinion, which though advanced by the despairing enemies of African freedom, and whispered perhaps, not without effect, into the ears of His Majesty's Ministers, is a mere unsupported dogma, and is at war with all the experience of mankind.

Should this brief attempt to disperse the mist of prejudice which hangs over the dawn of the new state, be unsuccessful, my practical conclusions, let it be again observed, depend not upon a favourable estimate of the character of the Indigenes; or on the hope of their future prosperity. Supposing them to relapse into anarchy and barbarism, they will, I admit, be less formidable enemies than I have imagined, and less desirable allies : But it is still wise to secure their amity, while they have advantages to impart; prudent to avert their enmity, while they have power to annoy; and necessary to prolong and perpetuate their separation from France, in whose hand, whether united or divided among themselves, whether civilized or barbarous, they would be most formidable instruments, and certain occasions of mischief.

Here,

Here, Sir, I might fairly take my leave, did not a sense of moral, as well as patriotic duty, irresistibly force upon me another important topic.

There is a subject, a most momentous and opprobrious one, which stands not indeed in any necessary connection with my argument, but upon which when recommending measures of West Indian policy, it is impossible not to reflect, and would be criminal to be silent.

The Slave Trade! How does that dreadful name dishearten the patriot hopes of an Englishman, who knows its horrors, and who has seen its pernicious effects! Could I forget, or doubt, that, " Verily, and indeed, there is a God who governs the earth;" I still could not sincerely hold forth the hope of a result finally beneficial to my country, from the measure recommended in these sheets, or from any other scheme of policy however wise, while that pestilent iniquity is cherished. It would be like promising prosperity to a prodigal, from arrangements of domestic economy, while he refused to forsake the gaming table or the race course; or health to a dropsical drunkard from medicine, while he persisted in the nightly debauch.

Yet I see my country still given up without remorse to the unbridled career of slave trading speculators. As if amorous of guilt and of ruin, we plunge deeper every day into that gulph of African blood.

Happy

Happy had it been, perhaps, if the veil of public ignorance, which for ages covered the deformities of that hideous commerce, had never been withdrawn ; for the monster instead of being cut off, as the first burst of honest indignation promised, has been more fondly nourished than before ; and fattened with fuller meals of misery and murder, into far more than his pristine dimensions. While the flagitious wickedness of the trade was exposed by the abolitionists, its gainful effects were blazoned by its defenders ; and the purblind avarice of the country was so strongly excited, that the man-merchant in an apparent defeat, obtained an actual triumph ; a triumph over national humanity ; and let me add, over all the moral decencies of legislative character. The pleadings of justice and mercy have served only, like the graceful supplications of violated beauty, to display more attractively the object of temptation ; and to inflame that cupidity, which their eloquence could not repress.

A momentary compunction was indeed excited in our senate, as well as in the country at large ; but its effect has been only to display in the foul relapse, and enormous extension of the crime, the low state of our public morals; and the fatal tendency of that vile principle of expediency, upon which immediate reformation was withheld.

Do these strictures, Sir, appear too strong?
Ask

Ask yourself then I entreat you, what would have
been said in the House of Commons, had an abolitionist ventured to predict in the debates of 1792,
events which have since happened, " that instead
" of finally terminating the Slave Trade within
" a few years, we should within that period dou-
" ble its annual extent; that instead of limiting
" the supply by the alleged necessities of our old
" sugar colonies, we should covet and acquire a
" large unsettled island within the tropics, and
" people it by that detestable commerce *; that
" we should even explore new receptacles for the
" miserable victims of our avarice, in a foreign
" territory; and send a hundred thousand slaves,
" to fertilize by British capital and credit the
" sickly regions of Guiana." Surely, the speaker
would have been scoffed at as an absurd dreamer
who libelled the fair intentions of the Commons.
" Is thy servant a dog that he should do this?" the
indignant reply of a Jewish monarch to a pro-
phet upon a like occasion, might have expressed
the feelings of the house.

Such predictions, however, would have been an
inadequate expression of our subsequent inconsistency and guilt.

What use, Sir, are you now making of the late
Charib division of St. Vincent ? As to Trinidada,

* The Slave Trade, ever since our acquisition of Trinidada,
has been allowed in the ports of that island without qualifica-
tion or restraint

I forbear

I forbear, now fully to speak, what must, I fear, one day be spoken. While you hesitate upon the plan of colonization to be adopted in that new island, of which the fate is happily not yet committed to an assembly of planters, I will endeavour to hope in silence. But upon what principle, let me ask, is the importation of African negroes into this colony permitted without any modification or restraint, while we are taught to believe that the murderous old system of slavery is not meant to be finally planted there?

The conquest, or let me rather call it the acceptance, of Dutch Guiana, menaces a new aggravation of the guilt of Great Britain, and the miseries of Africa.

That this measure was grossly impolitic, must be evident to every well informed mind. Our cruizers, to the great encouragement of our naval service, would have captured and brought into our ports, at least four-fifths of all the produce exported from that country ; thereby checking the growth of settlements, which are a nuisance to the British planter, and leaving to our enemies the deathful charge of their interior defence. Instead of this, Demarara, Issequibo, and Berbice, are already taken again under the fostering wing of Great Britain. The Dutch, and the Anglo-Dutch planters, fondly rush into our arms, in order to be safe from our hostility; and to be nourished

again

again, as they doubtless hope, with British capital
and credit; as well as to enjoy the security during
war, of British navigation. In return, they gene-
rously allow and engage you to provide for their
internal safety; and to guarantee them against
the fearful tendencies of their having lately added
to their population a hundred thousand African
slaves.

Surinam too, if report may be credited, has
probably ere now condescended to change its
flag on the same advantageous terms: and here,
our regular troops, which we so easily recruit, and
can so well spare from European service, will
have frequent opportunities of gathering laurels,
in the unceasing war maintained by that colony
against the Maroon negroes of the interior. Perhaps the Dutch Assembly may be more civil than
that of Jamaica; and be gracious enough, while we
are at all the expence of life, to contribute a
little money for their own defence; since the
standing contribution to their own government
for the support of the Maroon war alone, was six
per cent. on all their produce.

How many regiments annually the sickly swamps
of that settlement may consume for us, I cannot
presume to estimate; but Demarara is said to
have furnished graves to almost the entire garrisons sent out to receive it at the last peace, con-
sisting

sisting of about twelve hundred Batavian regulars, in little more than a single year.

Could I with propriety here pursue this subject further, it would be easy to shew the cruel hardships imposed upon our own planters, by the diversion made by Guiana speculations, of such commercial capital as is usually invested in West Indian loans; the injustice of opening freely the British market during war to the produce of these foreign colonies ; and the extreme folly of suffering them to be improved and extended by subjects of this country.

But these considerations are not strictly within the scope of my present argument. I now wish to look to the inauspicious conquests in question, no further than as they, like the other facts to which I have referred, stand related to the Slave Trade ; and consequently to the plan of policy which it is the business of these sheets to recommend. If then, as these measures unhappily seem to threaten, the old maxims are still to prevail— if we are still, with insatiable avidity, to prosecute the Slave Trade, to every extent, and in every direction, to which the spirit of gambling speculation may invite—if to this end, we are to open new lands, plant new colonies, and manure with British capital and credit, every foreign and rival soil between the tropics, where slave buyers can
be

be found---if I say we are to persist in this infatuated and atrocious career; the advice which I have taken all this trouble to support is certainly not worth your attention.

In that case, it matters little whether you avert from our sugar colonies the evils which menace them from St. Domingo; for mischiefs more surely destructive are ripening in those new fields of blood ; and will soon be wafted by the wings of the trade wind upon them. It will profit us little in that case, to rescue our army from the hospitals of Jamaica; for graves sufficiently wide to contain the whole of it, are opening in Trinidada and Guiana.—It will be a fruitless work to stop by a wise policy the course of revolution at one end of the Charibbean Chain, for its electric shock will soon be transmitted from the other.

Nor is it necessary, as far as the welfare of our old colonies is concerned, to suppose, that the sudden introduction of another hundred thousand of Africans into those settlements, will produce in speedy insurrection its natural effect. The rivalship of those colonies, should they prosper, will be certain ruin to the old British planter, and destruction to his slaves.*

But,

* The author regrets that he must here abstain from the discussion of a most important topic. It might be demonstrated,

U

But, abstaining from the further consideration of these natural consequences of the Slave Trade, and omitting to state its obvious incompatibility with that permanent friendship which I would advise you to cultivate with the people of St. Domingo ; let me avow, before I conclude, the influence of still higher motives.—Yes, Sir ! however it may revolt the prejudices of many who regard the raising our eyes beyond second causes, as no part of political wisdom, I will freely confess, that I can hope no good result from the measure here recommended, or from any other precautions of national prudence, while we continue to defy the justice of Omnipotence, by the horrible iniquities of the Slave Trade.

I know the unequalled miseries inflicted upon myriads of the children of Adam, by that commerce ; I know the horrors of the system which it feeds and perpetrates ; I believe that, there is a righteous governor of the earth ; and therefore I

strated, from premises which even the West Indian Committee would admit, that the planters of the old islands must be ruined, if the settlement of the cheap lands in these colonies, is further to be encouraged or allowed : and it is a plain corollary from this proposition, that slaves bound by mortgages to the soil, as the negroes in the islands almost universally are, must be gradually worked down and destroyed, in the fruitless but necessary attempt, to keep down by parsimony and exertion the interest of the growing incumbrances.

dare

dare not hope well of the fortunes of my country, while she stands with an impious obduracy, between the mercy of God, and the deliverance of Africa.

Nor are there symptoms wanting, which appear to develope a providential plan, for the relief of that much injured race, and the punishment of their oppressors.

In the wonderful events and coincidences which have planted, fostered, and defended, the liberty of St. Domingo, I seem to see that hand by which the fates of men and nations are directed. I seem to see it, in that strange train of public evils, which, since the first blaze of light revealed the full guilt of the Slave Trade, and since we rejected the loud call for reformation, have chastized our national obduracy. I seem to see it, in the dark clouds which now menace the domestic security, the idolised wealth, the happiness, and even the liberty and independency, of my country.

For that Satanic mind which is now suffered to sway the destiny of Europe, few are more inclined, in a natural view, than myself, to mingle contempt with abhorrence; but when I consider what instruments the Almighty has sometimes been pleased to employ in purposes of national vengeance, and when I think of the Slave Trade, I cannot wholly despise the menaces of our

haughty

haughty enemy, even upon British ground. I
can only exclaim—

> " ———— Non me tua fervida terrent
> " Dicta, ferox: Dii me terrent, et Jupiter hostis."

APPENDIX.

Extracted from THE SUN, *of Saturday,*
April 28, 1804.

St. DOMINGO.

LIBERTY OR DEATH!—NATIVE ARMY.

THE GENERAL IN CHIEF TO THE PEOPLE OF HAYTI.

" CITIZENS,

" IT is not enough to have expelled from your
Country the barbarians who have for two ages
stained it with blood; it is not enough to have
curbed the factions which, succeeding one another, by turns sported with a phantom of Liberty
which France exposed to their eyes. It is become
necessary, by a last act of National Authority, to
ensure for ever the Empire of Liberty in a Country which has given us birth. It is necessary to

X

deprive

deprive an inhuman Government, which has hitherto held our minds in a state of the most humiliated torpitude, of every hope of being enabled again to enslave us.—Finally, it is necessary to live independent or die. Independence or Death! Let those sacred words serve to rally us, let them be signals of battle and of our re-union.

Citizens, Countrymen, I have assembled on this solemn day, those courageous Chiefs who, on the eve of receiving the last breath of expiring Liberty, have lavished their blood to preserve it.—These Generals who have conducted your efforts against tyranny, have not yet done enough. The French name still darkens our plains; every thing recalls the remembrance of the cruelties of that barbarous people. Our laws, our customs, our cities, every thing bears the mark of the French. What do I say? the French still have a footing in our island, and you believe yourselves free and independent of that Republic, which has fought all nations it is true, but which never conquered those who would be free! What, victims for fourteen years of our credulity and forbearance! conquered not by French armies, but by the canting eloquence of the Proclamations of their Agents! When shall we be wearied with breathing the same air with them?—What have we in common with that bloody-minded people? Their cruelties, compared to our moderation, their colour to ours, the extension of seas which separate us, our
avenging

avenging climate, all plainly tell us they are not
our brethren; that they never will become such;
and if they find an asylum among us, they will
still be the instigators of our troubles and of our
divisions. Citizens, men, women, young and old,
cast round your eyes on all parts of this island;
seek there your wives, your husbands, your bro-
thers, your sisters—What do I say? Seek your
children—your children at the breast, what is become of them? I shudder to tell it—the *prey of
vultures.* Instead of these interesting victims, the
affrighted eye sees only their assassins—tigers still
covered with their blood, and whose terrifying
presence reproaches you for your insensibility and
your guilty tardiness to avenge them—what do
you wait for to appease their manes? Remember
that you have wished your remains to be laid by
the side of your fathers—When you have driven
out tyranny, will you descend into their tombs,
without having avenged them? No, their bones
would repulse yours; and ye invaluable men, in-
trepid Generals, who, insensible to private suffer-
ings, have given new life to liberty, by lavishing
your blood, know that you have done nothing if
you do not give to the nations a terrible, though
just example, of the vengeance that ought to be
exercised by a people proud of having recovered
its liberty, and zealous of maintaining it. Let us
intimidate those who might dare to attempt de-
priving us of it again:—let us begin with the
French

Freneh; let them shudder at approaching our
shores, if not on account of the cruelties they have
committed, at least at the terrible resolution we
are going to make, to devote to death, whatsoever
native of France should soil with his sacrilegious
footstep this territory of Liberty.

" We have dared to be free—let us be free by
ourselves and for ourselves; let us imitate the
growing child; his own weight breaks his leading
strings, which have become useless and troublesome to him in his walk. What people have
fought us? what people would reap the fruits of
our labours? and what dishonourable absurdity
to conquer to be slaves!

" *Slaves*, leave to the French Nation this qualifying epithet, they have conquered to be no
longer free—let us walk on other foot-steps; let
us imitate other people, who, carrying their solicitude into futurity, and dreading to leave to posterity an example of cowardice, have preferred to
be exterminated, rather than to be erased from
the list of free people. Let us, however, take
care, lest our spirit of proselytism should destroy
our work—let our neighbours breathe in peace—
let them live peaceably under the shield of those
laws which they have framed for themselves; let
us beware of becoming revolutionary fire-brands
—of creating ourselves the Legislators of the Antilles—of considering as a glory the disturbing the
tranquillity of the neighbouring Islands; they have
                                              not

not been, like the one we inhabit, bathed in the
innocent blood of their inhabitants—they have no
vengeance to exercise against the authority that
protects them; happy never to have experienced
the plague that has destroyed us, they must wish
well to our posterity.

" Peace with our neighbours; but accursed be
the French name—eternal hatred to France; such
are our principles.

" Natives of Hayti—my happy destiny reserves
me to be one day the Sentinel who is to guard the
idol we now sacrifice to. I have grown old fighting for you, sometimes almost alone; and if I have
been happy enough to deliver to you the sacred
charge confided to me, recollect it is for you at
present to preserve it. In fighting for your liberty, I have laboured for my own happiness; before it shall be consolidated by laws which insure
individual liberty, your Chiefs whom I have assembled here, and myself, owe you this last proof
of our devotedness.

" Generals and other Chiefs, unite with me for
the happiness of our Country; the day is arrived,
the day which is to perpetuate our glory and our
independence.

" If there exist among you a lukewarm heart,
let him retire, and shudder to pronounce the oath
which is to unite us. Let us swear to the whole
world, to posterity, to ourselves, to renounce
France for ever, and to die rather than live under

its

its dominion—to fight till the last breath for the Independence of our Country.

" And ye, People, too long unfortunate, witness the oath we now pronounce : recollect that it is upon your constancy and courage that I depended when I first entered the career of Liberty to fight despotism and Tyranny, against which you have been struggling these last fourteen years; remember that I have sacrificed every thing to fly to your defence —Parents, Children, Fortune, and am now only rich in your Liberty. That my name has become a horror to all people, the friends of Slavery and Despots, and Tyrants only pronounce it, cursing the day that gave me birth; and if ever you refuse or receive in murmuring the Laws, which the protecting angel that watches over your destinies shall dictate to me for your happiness, you will merit the fate of an ungrateful people. But far from me this frightful idea : you will be the guardians of the liberty you cherish, the support of the Chief who commands you.

" Swear then to live free and independent, and to prefer death to every thing that would lead to replace you under the yoke; swear then to pursue everlasting Traitors, and the enemies of your Independence.   J. J. DESSALINES."

" *Head Quarters, Gonaives,*
" *1st Jan.* 1804, *1st Year of Independence.*"

Since the above proclamation was sent to press, the author has received the following extract from a Boston a Boston newspaper just arrived, which seems to place it out of doubt that vindictive executions, at least, if not massacres, have really taken place in St. Domingo.

Extract from a Boston Newspaper of the 5th of May 1804.

" The Governor of Hayti has directed the publication of the following Arretés in the papers of the United States:

" The Governor General considering that there still remains in the Island of Hayti individuals who have contributed either by their guilty writings, or by their sanguinary accusations, to the drowning, suffocating, assassinating, hanging, and shooting of more than 60000 of our brethren, under the inhuman government of Leclerc and Rochambeau : considering that every man who has dishonoured human nature by prostituting himself with enthusiasm to the vile offices of informers, and of executioners, ought to be classed with assassins, and delivered up without remorse to the sword of justice ; decrees as follows:

" 1. Every commandant of division shall cause to be arrested within their respective commands, the persons who are or shall be known to have taken an active part in the different massacres and assassinations ordered by Leclerc or Rochambeau.

" 2. Before proceeding to the arrest of any individual (as it often happens that many are innocent, who nevertheless may be strongly suspected)

we

we order each commandant to make all necessary enquiries for procuring proofs; and above all, not to confound with true and faithful reports those denunciations too frequently suggested by envy and hatred.

" 3. The names and sirnames of persons executed shall be inserted in a list, and sent to the General in Chief, who will make them public, in order to inform the nations of the world that although we grant an asylum and protection to those who act candidly and friendly towards us, nothing shall ever turn our vengeance from those murderers who have bathed themselves with pleasure in the blood of the innocent children of Hayti.

" 4. Every chief, who in contempt of the orders and unalterable will of government, shall sacrifice to his ambition, to his hatred, or to any other passion, any individual whose guilt shall not have been previously well ascertained and proved, shall undergo the same punishment which he shall have thus inflicted, and the property of every such unjust officer shall be confiscated, one half to the government, and the other half to the relations of the innocent victim, if any there may be in the island at the time of his death.

" DESSALINES."

Done at Gonaives, 29th of February,
True copy, B. Aimé, Secretary.

FINIS.

C. WHITTINGHAM, Printer, Dean Street.

For EU product safety concerns, contact us at Calle de José Abascal, 56–1°, 28003 Madrid, Spain or eugpsr@cambridge.org.